Gateway to the Fifth Dimension

Book One

Ivan Teller

www.IvanTeller.com

This channeled text is brought to you by the fifth dimension.

CONTENTS

About The Book

Gateway to the Fifth Dimension Book 1 is a channeled text from various spirit guides and high councils in the spirit world. Call this a gift from the future. This book is one volume and just a small amount of material that is out there. Call this a window into the unknown.

Knowledge is knowledge, and no matter what your belief system, the information here is to help with your awareness of the unknown – the unknown to be known and to grow beyond the modern teachings and to graduate from this level of consciousness. And what exactly is the graduation? As you heal the third dimension and leave the problems of this current age and bring in higher dimensional knowledge. So you can build ships that can travel through light. Build new technologies that can assist with your telepathic abilities. A new voice of reason will emerge.

To open portals and to see them clearly. To touch them and to feel the outer rim into other realities. Humanity is awakening into a new level of consciousness that might seem scattered right now. But in the future, all will be clear.

This book is a send off of the third dimension. A healing energy and an awareness of what the human is capable, with abilities to stop time and to travel through it. Your astral self will see other realities and timetables of what is to come.

Everyone on this planet has an extraterrestrial connection. It's time to embrace the unknown and to travel into the knowledge you know as in infinite light. Exploring infinite dimensions, explaining your reality even more. Reaching out to infinite wisdom that will breathe life into your current reality. The idea is to change your reality for the better.

About Ivan Teller

Back in 2011 is when I had my awakening. Even before then I knew there was a spirit world and had some understanding of psychics. Maybe not the easiest life. Actually, in all honesty, it wasn't easy and still isn't.

Connecting to the spirit world and unlocking the third dimension is no easy task. Our current world has always been going through a healing phase. This next phase that will unravel for the next hundred years will change the way humanity sees itself.

I met a tarot card reader through a friend, and soon after, the past life aggression connected to my spirit guides and I began to understand the spirit world, and this was in 2011. During that process I was possessed by a dark entity and cleared it, and in 2014 discovered I had another dark entity attached to me since I was a child. That entity was disconnected, and ever since, I've been very aware of the unseen world.

Welcome to the real world.

Humanity chooses to look the other way while being entertained by horror movies and alien movies, not understanding the spirit world is speaking to everyone.

Humanity isn't really a child, but it chooses to act like one and look the other way. Always an excuse it's not ready, and that is true. How long can humanity turn its head–going to theme parks that carry alien and elemental energies from agartha?

The fundamentals of what is going on is not to say, 'I told you so.'

The idea is to let go of the old world and open a new one. Understand your psychic abilities that you use on a daily basis.

On March 15, 2015, I did my first channeling.

Just by following a step-by-step audio on how to channel, after the first try I got my main spirit guide through. That guide is Ulysses that I later fired. Fortunately most people won't have to fire their guides. Come to think of it, he was removed by the high councils for doing such a bang-up job.

So I guess the higher councils have blinders on because Ulysses has been a pain from the very start. Gotta love those soul contracts. About a year after this, I fired all my guides. I've had women manipulate my guides saying I'm their soulmate. Come on, give me a break.

Fired the guides a few times. So if anyone manipulates your guides and says your guide agrees I'm your soulmate, it's time to get rid of that person and fire the guides.

By the way, the 15th is the Ides of March, the day Julius Caesar was murdered. Have to admit I'll never forget that date.

For the next few years, getting used to channeling was a task all in its own. And how does one do this? Channel every single day in a webinar. Have a bunch of strangers ask you questions and take the highway into the future.

After the first channeling I knew to record everything I do. YouTube, as shady as it might be, upload everything and hope for the best.

The reason channeling aliens made sense is because since I was a kid, I was very creative but was rejected by all creative outlets. I learned how to write screenplays even if I don't follow the rules.

Before I did my first channeling, I was finishing up writing a book, and you never know–that might be published one day.

So frustrating to feel you fit in on a world you kind of despise.

In truth, I feel nothing for this world. I know there is good here, but I couldn't care less about its rules or its entertainment. I guess you can say I feel I can do better.

For right now, channeling is the direction and helps humanity move from the old ways of life.

I come from a place where aliens are created. You can say this is the angelic realms and beyond.

To be honest, you'd be surprised how many dark entities are incarnated on this earth. By dark entities I mean demons. And many think they know everything and connecting to aliens is too cute and fine and all. But there are beings here that are very tricky. And the world turns into fairies fighting demons, something you would see in a fantasy story.

I believe everyone is an angel. As for what kind of angel is another story. A lot of channelers are weak and give in to the manipulations. Just channel aliens and be cute about it.

Secretly, the deceivers are hidden because people aren't ready to see the truth.

Basically it's good against evil and unlocking the evil from humanity's consciousness.

Greetings Humanity

Greetings, humanity. The time is coming for the high-vibration transformation. Realize you are connected to the animal star people. The animal kingdom on your animal is no different than you.

As your vibrations heighten, the understanding of this will come more true to you. As of now, the majority of humans see animals as another species when, in fact, they are you and you are them. Most of you have been animals on your planet before a human incarnation.

Those who enjoy flying are usually from the flying insectoid races–always with wings and always ready to fly.

It is time for the human to reconnect to the universe. By doing this, expect the unexpected and realize many waves of change are on their way. In the past, your planet was plunged into darkness with no way out. Some of this is in your Bible, the book of Zechariah.

Your current darkness is the industrial revolution that has technology taking over your current lives. The birth of artificial intelligence was during your World War II. Humanity has to make a decision–to find what is truth in your life or continue to live the lie of the third dimension.

We realize many would rather not hear the truth and will believe whatever they what and call it truth. There are dimensions that will comfort those belief systems, and they will continue on that timeline of disbelief.

Comfort in the mind is no different than comfort food. Everyone wants to feel good. There is nothing wrong with that. But looking the other direction as others suffer is neglect of your fellow human beings.

Save yourself. Free your mind. Realize the darkness of your planet. Desire to look the other way. Live in comfort and forget the troubles of the world. Darkness prevails in your comfort. When you want to truly see the truth, the truth will come. You might have a great deal of disbelief at first. But ask for assistance during this transition into the unknown.

The reptilian manipulations are ending on your planet. Fires and strange global warming are on their way as the Earth transitions into the fourth dimension.

A strange world is on its way. The mysteries will continue to unravel as Egypt comes to life. The Atlantean knowledge is opening portals across your Earth. A great transition is near.

There will be a future when alien ships will be welcomed back into your lives. The animal kingdom will be more important to you.

You can say Earth is being disconnected from Planet X. The manipulations will be cleared and you will see Planet X with no problem. Yes, other worlds are causing difficulties on your planet. More of these beings were kicked off Earth but continued to cause trouble.

Saturn, Uranus, and Mars have been a mix of conflict on your world. Planet X is not seen in your solar system in your dimension. It's larger than your moon and can even replace your moon sometime in the future.

As you upgrade your vibrations, you will understand this. Heal Planet X and bring it closer to you. Yes, this is the Annunaki world. It will be seen as fantasy until your dimension is ready for it to be seen in your reality.

It is possible for your planet to advance its technologies in the next ten years, where the alien influence becomes more obvious. The Air Force already has these technologies but feel humans are not ready for it yet.

As you mature and know your surroundings more clearly, healing the hostility on your planet is what is needed most. Many of you are ready but more are not. There are too many activities within the third dimension that are too attractive to let go of. Most are not ready to let go.

Understand this, that many in the spiritual community want to control the fourth and fifth dimensions. You will see this as the ego spins out of control, wanting attention and thinking they are always right.

In four years you will see the great change occur.

Blessings

Gateway to the Fifth Dimension

The outer layer of your planet is protected by fifth dimension energies. Every human on your planet is a multidimensional being. Realizing these talents will assist with the realization you are not alone in the universe.

It's like taking off an old coat you have worn for centuries and realizing that phase of your life is over and you no longer need to think that it's cold outside. When the soul awakens to the fourth and fifth dimensions, weather on your world will no longer be needed.

This channeled text is a new kind of thinking, and we encourage everyone to practice channeling in some form of another. Realizing no one is the same will encourage you to go further into the unknown of your own vibration, which is your own universe.

Understanding outside the third dimensional thinking is not easy. The teachings of this planet are very third dimensional and very much needed as you graduate towards the next level of consciousness.

Do realize all information matters – no matter what. Helpful information takes all forms. Religion is a belief system for humans to realize spirituality. You can say religion is the growing pains of your world, showing that connecting to spirit won't be easy.

As you see, many souls enjoy the thrills of the third dimension. Your current reality is what we are speaking of. As you activate your consciousness to a higher frequency, you will slowly begin to understand the mysteries of the world. Graduating to the fourth dimension is a process that can cause the mind to wander back into negativity.

And negativity is there to hold you in the fourth dimension. As you reach out for higher knowledge, there are many beings on your planet who feel you have no business upgrading your reality. Growing up is hard to do.

Humanity on earth was, in some ways, forced into the third dimension. As with Atlantis, the world of the past came crashing down, and connecting with a spirit almost became impossible. You can look at Atlantis and Lemuria as heaven, if you like. A connection to the spirit world that made life so fulfilling; living for a thousand years and being able to do just about anything the mind can create.

The break down of humanity is the current discension that you are experiencing. Many souls aren't willing to let go of the third dimension. For some, there is nothing better than this current reality. This is home, and many souls are all for never having it change. Being materialistic and enjoying the perks of the modern world is just enough.

Hearing the tales about aliens brings a fascination. But connecting to the aliens in the physical is almost an impossible reality. Most humans don't even think about the outside world. For many of you, that's where you live. You live outside of earth and that is what you call home.

Fourth and fifth dimension energies are here to heal the current world reality.

One day, humans will be able to shift their vibration and be able to fly and walk through walls. Currently, humanity is slowly going through a culture shift. As more channelers enter the world arena, there won't be any stopping the fifth dimension energies.

Everyone in this world has the tools they need to live in this reality. Not all your powers will be activated as you would like. Some would like to activate their power and leave the earth right now.

Understand humanity needs your knowledge. Those that are dreading this reality need that dread of the higher energies to assist with the ascension. Call it a reminder. It's a blessing or a curse – that's up to you.

There are those that are aware of the higher dimensions and don't really want to be on earth. Your energies are needed for the ascension. Each negative attack shows you are opening the earth to the higher dimensions. You are gifting mother earth with your blessings. Mother earth asked you to be here. And most of you did say "no" at first; "I'll think about it" and a few thousand years went by.

You being here helps with the awakening to the higher spirit energies. Even if you don't understand everything, that is fine. Connect to higher energies that bring comfort to you. In five to ten years, humanity will be seeing the world as you see it. And when that happens, you're release from your contract will occur.

Do realize with spiritual development you are creating a new economy. Instead of money, you will use crystals. Activating each other will occur more frequently when the old ways of living are no longer needed.

Everyone is a gift to this planet.

Humanity realizing they can let go of their fears is not an easy transition. For many, fear is safety. It's a way of life that has been echoed throughout history. The Catholic Church has ingrained the ideas of fear for thousands of years. The challenge of this world is letting go of old ideas.

The elite are more than aware of those of you who wish to ascend from the manipulations of your current reality. The elite play on all sides to bring a divide. No one is perfect – you don't have to like everyone. Do realize there are forces here to divide you all and continue with the dream world of manipulation.

As you awaken to the higher energies, you are also tossing out the old contracts that created the third dimension. Not an easy contract to let go of, seeing how you have been born with it. Living through the menu items of life. Going to school and making your place in the world. Feeling empty wondering if this is all there is. As you expand your consciousness, you will see the manipulations are complex on your planet.

Is life a game? For some it is a game. It's a game of choice, you can say.

You came here to make a good life for yourself and your family.

For many, a good life is connecting to the higher dimensions; connecting to aliens and feeling free, where you can travel the universe without complication. Connecting to the universe is freeing yourself.

Understand – you live in several realities at once. The physical reality being the most difficult.

Earth the child planet doesn't make it easy for the aliens. The child planet is easy to manipulate and a great challenge for the universe. Humanity on earth can't seem to get it together, can it? There is starvation on the planet, with false religions with a distorted view on life. And if you are wondering, who on earth will be the hardest to ascend into the higher dimensions?

Religion is an anchor of twisted belief systems that open up the realms of lower astral. False ideas of death and what is of moral. Darkness lives within modern day religion, unfortunately. Not to say all religion is negative and a false energy.

With modern religious ideas, you are dead before you are alive. You come into this world to obey the word of God. The god of your current religion is here to imprison your soul on this earth. Enjoy happiness as a child as long as you can. The real world will shut the joy down and put you to work.

The idea of modern religion is to trap you on this world. Trap you into this dimension and it has worked out very well throughout the ages. Trap you into the ideas of how to be a human. Welcome to the prison planet.

Understand – prisoners don't think for themselves.

Modern religion has set up guidelines of how to be human and what morality is. You must comply or be seen as an outcast.

Spirituality should be the freedom to think whatever you want. No restrictions as to your morals and also what gender you choose. Atlanteans had the ability to change genders. Finding comfort in who you are will become the new normal.

Religion is a Annunaki control system. Humanity, as it descended into third dimension, wanted to stay there, and so the invention of religion was built. The founders of all the religions are alien connected.

Aliens out of control, you may say. As we said, the earth child was giving the alien parents a hard time. When humanity disconnected from the spirit, the idea of god was lost. The inner god was forgotten and replaced with aliens.

False gods interacted with your planet, with Annunaki influencing parents into marrying their own children and having children. Arradic breeding practices were known throughout the ancient world, and many were leaders of the ancient religions.

The ancient priests couldn't be married to their mothers or have children anymore. Some forbade any kind of sexual relationship all together. There are different reasons why priests don't marry. Look at the modern priests and their behavior. It's very Annunaki of them to prey on children. For them, this is the only way of life. The Catholic religion was founded by the Annunaki, so you must follow their practices.

The elite follow these practices without a problem. But they are unseen and can do whatever they want. The priests have the same desires. The priests are programming humanity how to think. The source is connected to the Annunaki. So the desire to prey on children should hopefully make more sense.

Annunaki can handle marrying and having children with their own children but humans can't. We also want to make clear the Catholic religion is connected to many alien beings. To continue the control over humanity, the Annunaki is a major influence.

6

Some of the priests receive a high from the aliens and become an Annunaki and not even know it. The Pope dressing up like a fish is very Annunaki. The Illuminati is based on Annunaki ideas. The priests and the bishops are the children of the ideas.

They are channeling information they don't understand. They just want to be connected with god and live a good life. Annunaki is god to them, and channeling those energies makes one not even human. Alien influence is everywhere, you just need to look at it from a different perspective.

Not all Anunnaki are like this. Those that want power over the people will do anything for it. Live an unconventional life. Illuminati Annunaki are connected to the dark forces that create your timelines of deception; connected to your educational system, the media and the basic functionality of living your life. The idea is to keep you in the system of control until your death. The idea is to trap you on this planet and feed off of your energies.

Many souls have been defeated on this planet. Thinking they can withstand the Annunaki manipulation and not fall for it. Some fall for the manipulations and even become bullies. They become successful and even become a CEO of a company. Thinking they conquered this world and, in truth, that isn't the case. They were conquered instead, and even carrying out the manipulation. It does happen often. Because they are so used to success. When incarnated into this world, they connect to the false ideas of success. Some even get trapped on this world for centuries, continuing to be in leadership positions, keeping the blindfold over humanity.

False ideas of success will continue to break down during the ascension. Reptilians want to keep the mental grid of manipulation over the mind's eye. The idea of humanity breaking down is true in some sense. The old ideas of living are breaking down as spiritual ideas connecting to the higher dimensions increase.

Darkness on this planet weakens as spiritual understanding increases. The rapid growth of higher dimensional understanding will increase. You are all teachers, and slowly you will find the teacher within. Higher self-teachings are never easy because of the ideas of the old world.

As you find the satisfaction of being an infinite being, and understand that anything is possible, your spirit can do and go anywhere. Trust yourself and will see the inner spirit within flow even faster with light.

Atlanteans Are Angels

Quick note: When receiving this download about angels being Atlanteans, a dark elf appeared in my energy field–a very powerful dark elf that can shut down the energy of a reptilian or any other alien being, except an angelic energy.

Where this download came from is, the being is a fallen angel by the name of Dark Michael, an angelic energy that wishes to change his vibration from darkness to light. More details on this will be channeled later.

From the beginning:

Higher-dimensional humans do exist on your world. The question is, do you see them or not? The angelic presence on this world is what is keeping earth alive. For anyone to say that the positive is disorganized and useless might want to look again.

Angels have Atlantean powers. Humanity went to sleep to be in the chamber of dissolution to expand and upgrade their consciousness. Let's put it this way. When the Atlanteans were tested, they instantly lost. The majority fell to the dark side.

How to prove this. Just look at your modern world. What gets the most attention, positive or dark? An action movie with extreme violence makes millions of dollars and breaks records. Violence in video games and negativity in music is at a record high.

This has nothing to do with manipulation. The human is exploring their own darkness as you can see. Yes, there is some manipulation, but you still can decide on what you like and dislike. And negativity in the media has a lot of strength.

Drama on the news gets the best ratings.

Humanity is slowly moving away from negativity, but it's up to the individual. It's not easy to assist a world that is drowning in negativity and with only a few willing to leave that aspect of life. Some spiritual workers can be very positive in their profession, but in their daily life they are the exact opposite.

The angelic timeline was created for higher-dimensional beings. When humanity lost its way, the founders of Atlantis disappeared as humanity dropped to the lower vibrations. A positive grid was created around the earth called the angelic realm.

Angels, Atlantis, and angelic realms do sound the same, don't they? You add the word Archon to this also and you get a better understanding of your founding.

Archons founded humanity on earth. They themselves are several different beings in one. Yes, they were assisted by the Creators and Elohim. The Creators are a mix of all beings that pull from God source energy.

Creating a planet from source–God is connecting to the creative consciousness of all beings. Universes are part of creation also. Your current universe is a door to other universes. Earth is a thousand universes mixed into one planet. That's why it's so dense.

The arts on your planet, most of them come from another universe. Your current universe is hollow depending on how you look at it. Have you ever wanted to explore this universe after leaving earth? Or do you want to go to another universe?

You've been to earth, which is a thousand universes. Why bother to continue in this universe?

You've seen it all here. Well, you felt it. Doesn't feel too good, does it? So dense because other universes want in, like a shopping mall with store after store constantly being crammed into a small space.

The Sirians, Pleiadians, etc. wanted the Archon experience and incarnated into their energies and created the human on earth. After the feline and reptilian wars, humans started appearing on earth.

The Archon alien disappeared during this time. You can say took a break as the creation process continued with the human. Archons were not called Archons during this time. For some aliens, it was a mystery species that carried no name.

When Atlantis began to fall into darkness, the Archon made their appearance again. There are different stages of this. But they were usually never seen as humanity was being developed on earth.

Reptilians played a major role in the human creation along with Pleiadians, Sirians, and a few thousand other species. The correct number of species connected to the human isn't truly known in your dimension. Even higher dimensions aren't sure completely.

Some aliens that are channeled are here to sugarcoat the truth of your higher-dimensional reality, as humanity begins to realize there is more than just lovable aliens and all kinds of various beings you can connect to.

There is an instant fear and an understood knowledge that humanity is just a small seed to the larger picture. Humanity is needed to advance other alien species such as elephant and feline. The Atlanteans were being manipulated by multiple alien beings and couldn't handle the manipulation at their rung of power.

Destroying the aliens was almost accomplished on earth.

Some of the aliens manipulating humans were brought down to third dimension as well–the snake and the insects to name a few. The feline and the elephant were not the nicest alien beings.

Annunaki joined the soul collective to incarnate on earth. Many became bankers and continued their manipulations. The Annunaki is an extension of the Archons, like a sister race. They continue to believe they know better.

The Annunaki became Atlanteans and then the Atlanteans became angels.

The fallen angels had wings and were manipulating humanity as the vibrations lowered across the earth. The positive angels acquired wings to heal the darkness done by the fallen angels.

The connection between angels and the Atlanteans.

The angels are the Atlanteans that did not lower their vibrations. The archangel energies are enhanced Arcturian and Atlantean energies combined. To continue in the higher levels, Arcturians are constantly assisting the higher realms while assisting with humanity in the lower dimensions.

All alien species have a combined effort, with the Arcturians as one of the highest alien energies that connect to the human race. Elohim is a high frequency also that combines with the Atlantean and Arcturian timelines.

Earth is connected to alien worlds with timelines.

The humans were abused through their creation process. And to be clear, human wasn't the most clear experience for this planet. Thousands of other species were experimented on before the human was the final call.

Imagine bird humans, feline humans, canine humans that were created on earth and now live on other worlds. Some are happy with their genetics and some are not. Wonder why humanity is so self-destructive?

There are many alien beings that do not want humans on this planet. They want you off the earth and destroyed. So the heavy energies you feel are the weight of being alive on earth. One of the reasons why it's so dense is because some beings want you out of here altogether.

Talk about pressuring you to leave.

Humanity is pressured to self-destruct. Look at the violence on this planet and look at the sporting events as an example. Violence is acted upon if a sports event is won or lost. Using violence to show happiness is a manipulation.

Alcohol and cigarettes shut you down from spirit. Food can also, but with alcohol you become uneven with your higher self and and drift off.

During the fall of Atlantis, vortexes were created for the higher realms. This was for higher-level Atlanteans to coexist with humans. The angelic realm always existed. This dimension was for Atlanteans to assist humanity on a higher level.

The illuminati have a similar dimension all to themselves.

These dimensions interconnect. You can say this is the control room for earth. These higher-dimensional beings called Atlanteans have a strong connection to the spirit world where they dictate what happens on earth.

They open a door to the spirit world for reincarnation to continue, but they say what goes.

Digest that one for a minute.

The spirit world is connected to earth, yes. You can call this the guardian dimension, where some of these beings are 30 feet tall. They connect to the spirit world and once again say what goes—similar to how Zeus and the gods operate.

The only difference is, this is unseen and not as abusive.

You can call this the guardian dimension or the archangel dimension. This is where your timelines are put together. So basically, the archangels assist with your timeline development, and the archangels are the new gods that ascended from Greek ancient antiquity.

There are accounts of people who, when visiting the spirit world, see ancient Greek architecture. They entered into the real Atlantis. The ancient world you see in ruins is alive and well in the guardian dimension.

Those ancient sites are there for healing and realize this reality goes on forever, meaning all of earth is here. If you are from India, you wish you will connect to an India spirit world, which is connected to all spirit worlds. Everything is connected and there are no borders and no divides

The True Awakening

Much gratitude to you all for being on this journey. This Earth's ascension process is connected to your energies. A high frequency of knowledge will soon be known. The understanding of your existence will find more meaning. The joys of life are yours. And don't forget to keep it simple. The doorway to your soul essence can be found. The magic of connecting to spirit is simple. A silence of the mind. A quiet place is wonderful. Now hear us.

This is a message from spirit.

What is happening now? The real question is, what is really happening on this Earth today? Is it negative reptilians manipulating the Earth's consciousness? Yes, but there is so much more happening. There is darkness here. But don't forget, you are the light.

As the human awakens to the true Earth, you will begin to see Archons in the skies. Dark forces continue to keep the human consciousness trapped in this three-dimensional prison. But those days are coming to an end. The new human is being born. The Atlantean human is awakening from its coma.

You can say life is a simulation and you are its players. Humanity is being played by very sophisticated beings that have a wicked sense of humor. It's not just reptilians, Archons, and Annunaki; there is so much more. The human consciousness will soon come to the realization that you are not alone. Ever wonder why life doesn't make much sense? Ever wonder why life is a mystery? It's a mystery because the beings controlling your society do not want you to know about them.

You are not to know you are being played. There are dark entities that empower themselves because the human doesn't believe they exist. It's time to understand this is an alien world and the darkness needs to be released.

Positive alien beings are assisting us in our ascension. For some of us, that is easy to understand. It's all easy for us to understand. But for the mass population, this is all very hard to believe. The world can switch over in a week or maybe even a day if the entire population realizes we are not alone, and that we have been mind-manipulated by negative beings.

Call them master manipulators or whatever you want to call them. In the end, it's game over. It's time for the world to wake up. Every member of this planet is an alien being. Those who deny the truth continue playing the game under the master manipulation plan. The more you understand we are being manipulated and it's time to end the hoax, the sooner we can ascend to the fourth and fifth dimensions and beyond.

Instead of waiting for an alien spacecraft to arrive, just look around you. We are not alone and those aliens you are waiting for to land are here with us now in another dimension. Our friends are here to protect us. Some are Lyran felines, Zeta Greys, Arcturians, Sirians, and positive reptilians, just to name a few.

Still don't believe it? Look at the animals on our planet. Those are the aliens you are looking for. Look at your dog, cat, and insectoids roaming around. It's time for humanity to wake up to the obvious truth all around us. Once our eyes awaken, the spaceships will arrive. Once we put down those guns and see the good in each other, we will experience our ascension to the new world.

Even those in the spiritual communities are not truly ready for alien contact. Can you imagine having a positive conversation with a six-foot insectoid? Or how about a humanoid reptilian or feline? Most people would be scared out of their minds. But this is where we are heading. Alien contact is right around the corner. And that corner can be a few years or a few thousand years. It's up to humanity. The future of the Earth is up to us. If you want a positive timeline you can have it. No, more worries of financial meltdowns or world wars. The awakening begins right now.

This is a brief overview of what is happening now.

The Dogstar

The Dogstar started this Earth. Your planet is influenced by millions of worlds. The Arcturians, Eloheim, and so many other beings brought energies from other worlds to your planet. Your oceans were started with light. The God consciousness influenced this Earth's formation from the very beginning.

Planet Earth, as you know it, is connected to other worlds in your galaxy. The consciousness of this galaxy gave your planet its final formation. There is never just one creator but several. The spirit world consciousness wanted a planet of great challenge. A soul challenger. There are other worlds similar to this. But Earth is a place of the unknown—where knowledge is lost and reinvented, where the soul forgot it even existed.

The idea of soul energy does not truly exist in mainstream thinking—hinted on, but it's not mainstream, meaning you don't see people on a daily basis speaking about their soul, about their astral travels or that they had an out-of-body experience. You can't say this without being laughed at. What this is called is Annunaki manipulation.

Those who laugh at you spiritually are under the manipulation of reptilian and other lower vibrational beings. It's time to awaken the soul. It's time to know your Earth's history.

With the fall of Atlantis was the fall of the soul. The knowledge of one's energy spirit was lost. And that is when this new journey began.

There are creatures here to keep you from remembering yourself. Now is the time to remember those creatures and the soul contracts you have with them: Archons, reptilians, and Annunaki to name a few. To break those contracts is to free yourself. Ask for an end to those contracts if they cannot be fully broken. Activate your intentions. Clear your mind and rebuild your life.

Now for an understanding of darkness.

Look at your world today. When you turn on the television, phone, or tablet and see the violence of your planet, even your violent entertainment, that should tell you something. That should tell you maybe you are not being told the true story.

To begin, many authors of literature predict the future or set the future agendas. Some authors predict technology transformations soon to come. And there are others who set the negative agenda such as school shootings and a dystopian existence, sexual situations that lead to violence and inner pain that blocks the soul from truly growing. There are Annunaki agendas to brings couples together who will later create a child to be abducted in a future time.

The modern times of your world are riddled with violence and confusion. Why is this all happening? It's happening because you created a contract with your creator to come to this world and to fulfill your mission, whatever it might be, to live in a world saturated with morbid conditions.

When Atlantis was destroyed, that set the agenda for this world to be attacked and infiltrated by lower vibrational beings. Atlantis did not survive the test of manipulation. And now you have a prison planet where the word 'soul' means nothing, where human life means nothing, where the human is seen as trash.

This might be harsh, but it is true. Human life on your planet or life in general is not treated very well. With poverty and homelessness running rampant, the idea to turn this around is not an easy task to do. The condition of Mother Earth is also a sign of low-vibration attacks.

When Atlantis was destroyed, the call-out for lower vibrational beings was open. You can call this an experiment or a life choice. The Atlanteans could not hold their vibration forever. There were lessons to be learned. You can say the Atlanteans had a weakness and it needed to be healed, a flaw within the human race. And understand at this time the Atlanteans were of fourth and sixth density.

Ancient Atlanteans were genetically connected to spirit in a way that offered a new creation experiment, a new kind of human never seen before, with talents and abilities that were only seen at a twelve density of existence. The Earth human mastered an advancement never seen before. That advancement caused problems over time.

At a fifth density, Atlanteans began to think they were gods. This godlike power caused destruction. You see the Greek gods in your history. That should give you an idea of how that twisted mentality influenced your society over time. Ancient Greek gods were Atlanteans that are tied to your Illuminati.

One time in your history they did show themselves. One of many times it should be said. Egyptian gods were not that much different. The Egyptian gods caused much DNA influences that lowered the frequency of humanity. The Greek gods mostly treated humanity like children.

Enough about that—back to forgotten ancient knowledge.

The Lemuria were at a sixth or seventh density depending on the being. They were more psychic, and the offspring are the Native Americans. The more advanced Lemurians traveled to the Americas North and South. Incas and Mayans were a mix of Atlanteans and Lemurians.

The Atlanteans were at a fifth and sixth density. But their powers were of a twelfth-density being. They had physical bodies, but they can transmit to other dimensions without a problem. They were godlike and influenced the Annunaki. The Earth human was unlike any alien being before it.

Wonder why? The Atlanteans could manipulate their own DNA from aging with crystals and other technologies. This ageless human was unlike anything before its time. So once the Atlanteans lost their powers due to low-vibration influences, the knowledge was lost with them.

The human Atlantean had a DNA codex that could not be replicated easily. Such a powerful species of human with so many flaws such as lacking a moral compass. The perfect human had a dark side never seen before. You see it today in your modern world. All that rich power created a darkness that was wicked beyond other alien beings.

The Atlanteans lived in paradise and advanced their capabilities using advanced technologies from other alien species. Over thousands of years their flaws became more implied. Basically they couldn't handle this power forever.

The Lumerians were more connected to nature. You can call them the dolphin or fish people. They had a love affair with the land. The Atlanteans were in love with humanity and creation, crystal energies that helped with genetic engineering, a scientific understanding that was always wanting to learn. As they began to learn about themselves, they saw their flaws.

The Atlanteans were not as immortal and perfect as they thought. This imperfection was manipulated by the Annunaki and the reptilians. And during this time also you can say the Sasquatch decided to go on their own. During this time the Dogman separated from the Atlanteans also.

During the time of Atlantis was a place of diversity of different species. The frog, feline, and the canine were in humanoid form. The bird people or Carian races were here also in humanoid form. As the human separated from the aliens and became more ego-controlled, the fall of Atlantis began to emerge.

So many different types of Atlantean beings, and the human wanted to be the master race, the reason being this human Atlantean had a weakness. And that weakness began a war on all other alien races. The Atlantean wars began with a separation. The toxic nature of the negative Atlanteans caused a divide and went on for thousands of years. The human Atlanteans wanted the Earth for themselves. Under their control the reptilian manipulations were and are still running through the veins of selfish power.

The Arab people are the fallen Atlanteans. The manipulations moved fast. First the Annunaki used the humans to empower themselves over other races. The Arab world became at one time the rulers of the Earth.

After the fall of Atlantis, the Arab world destroyed itself. As the third density increased its lower energies, the alien vibrations deteriorated. Aliens were seen as demons, and the human as you know it became the prominent race of being on this planet.

The aliens left their ancestors on Earth. The animal kingdom was left here to assist with the human experience.

To back track just a little, the early Atlanteans that were quickly corrupted by Annunaki and reptilian influences no longer felt they could connect to the council of Atlantis. The outsiders felt Atlanteans were doing it all wrong. The human should be the dominant species.

During the early times of Atlantis, all aliens were welcomed. Atlanteans were all forms of life. Another early Atlantean creation was the Zeta Grey. Other forms of Zetas were created during this time. There are various versions of Zeta, and this was one of them. The origins of the Zeta Grey is from Zeta Reticuli, but modifications and enhancements were added to their species.

Advancements were later corrupted, causing mutations, and much of the knowledge was lost also. The DNA was no longer as powerful as it was in the beginning. The DNA of the human being is a mystery to most alien races—the major reason for the abductions. The aliens want to reconnect to immortality. The Annunaki could not master immortality as the ancient Atlanteans did.

What was learned was that the human can be modified easily, which caused the downfall of Atlantis. The early Atlanteans that turned against humanity are connected to your modern Illuminati. There were many influences during that time. The early Martians that visited Earth found humans to be weak and arrogant.

When the early Atlanteans influenced by negative Annunaki beings could no longer co-exist with their fellow Atlanteans, they migrated to what is now known as Asia Minor. During this time many human races were created. The human race known as the black African and the Asian races were born. Zeta Grey influences are among the Asian races most. Pleiadian and Yahyel were known among the black races. The reptilian brain also became more prominent in humans. That wasn't always the case for humans.

Think of it this way. As the early humans influenced the world, many different kinds of races were created. Different colors and cultures were invented. Discovering a human with a reptilian brain was unheard of during the early years of Atlantis. This new breed of human was still very powerful, but also some were very ruthless.

There was no such thing as time during early Atlantis, but if you need to understand, Atlantis was at peace for around ten thousand years. Realize also the Earth was at a high vibration and full of different alien life and plant life for that matter. Giants also lived during this time as Agartha was everywhere on the planet–fairies, elves, and all kinds of elemental energies. Wonder why the spiritual and the elemental world has many influences? The elementals are part of everything when it comes to life. Ignoring nature is like ignoring yourself. This is another reason why humanity is at a such a low vibration. It forgets nature.

When the higher dimensions became poisoned by manipulation, nature was poisoned also. It was like the entire world became toxic. One of the most beautiful planets in the universe was now under siege, and at the time most beings didn't know why.

Aliens at this time had never seen a takeover like this before. The Atlanteans were fighting amongst each other. The new reptilian humans arrived to take over Atlantis and its power. These new humans were very powerful but also destructive. And this low-vibration influence took over the Atlantean way of life.

The Annunaki, reptilians, and Archons quietly influenced Atlanteans, quietly took over their minds, leading them to darkness. Give us your knowledge. We deserve it also. We deserve perfection.

The Atlanteans, to perfect perfectly, had to visit their dark side. Wonder why humans are so dark on your world? Darkness is not just being tested but understood. Every soul is experimenting with itself. If I'm influenced to do darkness, will I follow that darkness? Or will I follow the light and even forgive those influencers? Every day you learn something new, even if you don't recognize it. This world hits the soul with everything it's got. Every test you can think of, the soul at this moment is experiencing it.

Notice those with a lot of power waste their power, even destroy their careers for selfish reasons. Nothing is good enough for some souls. But eventually they will hit their breaking point. Okay, I got it. I can't handle a lot of power. I'll be poor in the next life.

Atlantis Connections Part 1

Reptilians want this world for themselves. They found a weakness in humans and exploited it, lowering the human vibration with thoughts of greed and selfishness. They showed humans riches and then took it away. Why do you think there is only a small percent who are wealthy on your world?

Reptilians programmed the human to want these riches. Gold, silver, and diamonds give the human false intentions to want these riches to be wealthy, disconnecting the human from spirit. Empty, low vibrations are being sent to the human to continue this low vibration strain.

Money is a low vibration. Those who are ruled by wealth will always follow it. And finding spirit will always be a difficulty. How do you survive without money? Tell yourself you will survive without money and everything will be fine. Build that timeline. It is possible to manifest.

"To be successful is to be rich with money" is incorrect.

After the low vibrations took over the planet, all knowledge of Atlantis was lost. The soul became ill with disease and third-dimensional energies. The Atlanteans decided to become obsessive and decided they should rule the Earth. A great war occurred, a war with everyone.

The reptilians put little effort into taking over Atlantis once the Atlanteans became more egotistical. Selfish is probably a better word for it–discovering their own darkness, a new journey of the soul. The only way for this new journey to continue was to destroy themselves. At the time they did not see it like that.

The powerful Atlanteans of the Councils of Nine decided to defend themself from outsiders. Outsider Atlanteans were in some cases more advanced than the original Atlanteans as for genetics, also more attractive and smarter in the mind.

What caused the destruction of Atlantis? Many events happened one after the other. The Atlanteans, those in the high councils, became lost. They never wanted war, but Atlantis was attacked by outside forces. Third-dimensional ideas began to sink into the minds of the Atlanteans.

The attacks from outside sources were ideas. Fear of an invasion, fear that the Atlanteans might lose it all. The paradise island was only temporary.

The reptilians basically let the Atlanteans destroy themselves by starting mental wars with the peaceful race, giving them no choice but to fight back. Alien races watching the Atlanteans had no idea the Atlanteans would destroy themselves until it was too late.

The Alpha Draconians made sure to keep their activities quiet. Stay away from the Pleiadians, especially the Tall Blonde Nordics. The methods of the reptilians were already known and would be detected. The Earth humans, on the other hand, had no idea. They were told but never truly experienced a reptilian manipulation.

The soul of the Atlantean was powerful but also weak. Advanced as for science and technology but weak as for mental weakness–character manipulation, which did take years to break down. A paradise place with advanced thoughts and creativity, a moral dilemma–so much power, but there was something missing. How do they retain this power? In a high-stress environment, can the Atlanteans keep their cool and make the right decisions?

The soul of the Atlantean at that point had not been fully explored. Yes, they can be of a positive light, but what about darkness? Can they go into darkness and reconnect to the light? At that point it had not been explored before.

This was not casual conversation, but it was discussed by the councils. Could it be they could lose their power and not gain it back? The depths of this disconnection is possible. One again, thinking like this was unheard of but did occur in small circles.

Savagery was a possibility within the Atlanteans, but, at these high levels, never explored.

Until the Annunaki and reptilians began their mind alterations. you can be the only one with this power. Forget the others. You can be a god. You call this today the God Complex. As the manipulations continued, the brain function changed also with many Atlanteans. Their mind was becoming more reptilian. As experiments continued to improve Atlanteans, it was actually there to strike them down.

The Atlanteans left Atlantis to create new human species and be with the reptilians and Annunaki manipulators. These Atlanteans were male and female, and the females did have children with the Annunaki and reptilians.

Relationships with aliens and Earth humans is basically a love fest between the races. All forms of lovemaking were manifested. Lovemaking with alien insects was conducted also. It wasn't often, but if both parties were attracted to each other, arrangements were made. And yes, insect people do exist. As the human consciousness catches up, you will see for yourself.

As for the Archons, they reproduce in their own hive. When they mend with humans, they connect to your thoughts and remove your thoughts and add their own. There are cases when they reproduce with humans. Some are born as homicidal maniacs, astral infusion which can turn into a natural birth.

They can reproduce in third dimension, but it's forbidden. Erratic behaviors and deformities occur in the birthing process, same as the reptilians but can be much worse.

Archons are attracted to Arcturian energies. The high intellect is an energy from which they can learn. An Archon manipulation can transform a noteworthy scientist into a psychopath introvert. Arcturians are very connected to the scientists of your world and spiritualists. The Archon have infiltrated both as you can see.

With your modern religion, there is God, but it's a merciful God. With the scientific communities, there is no god, only science. With the Archon agenda it's very simple. Control the mind and turn it into a maze. The Archon influences complicated your way of thinking. And they can also interfere with Annunaki and reptilian agendas also. Archons can be seen as demons and also very powerful light angels.

Another reason why you have the archangels. Some of them are positive archangels. Archons are known to have wings because they connect to all species–the bird, insect, reptilian, and all forms of life. Reptilian pigs with an Archon influence can be troublesome on your world. They are no longer welcomed on your planet.

Notice Archon and Archangel in the same name context. It's because the positive Archon can be seen as one of the most powerful beings on your planet. Is Archangel Michael a positive Archon? Yes, he is. Through the flow of light of his soul, he has connected to all beings of light. He's been challenged in many lifetimes and lost himself. He lost the courage to be his true self, but after thousands of years of being tested, he has mastered eternal love.

You can say Archangel Michael is a double agent. He knows the light and also the dark. To fend off the dark, you must know it. To hold it and remove it, you must understand it. When you have a priest in your timeline clearing a demonic possession, the priest must understand darkness to remove and heal the darkness. Not to say you must be dark, but you must understand it so you yourself are not possessed. This is why understanding the dark is so important. Some run away from it.

Realize you can't always run. There is nothing to be afraid of. Those who run are afraid of the dark within themselves. Facing your own inner darkness shows a great amount of maturity. People who are here to do harm on your world are experiencing their darkness. To let it out and to grow, to be a dark being is one of the great experiences. Usually newer souls fall into this the easiest, but that's not always the case. Souls can lie in darkness for thousands or millions of years and beyond. But realize this also, you can always find the light. Many are not ready to see the light.

The battle between light and dark continues on your world. Darkness can bring in the rating, sell record albums and even books and movies. Letting go of this type of manipulation is no easy task.

Look at this even further. Think of going into darkness as similar to having a sex change. You are changing your frequency. That is all it is. It's just a new experience. When light runs away from darkness, darkness continues to chase it. When you face darkness, darkness no longer sees the joy with antagonizing you. Sometimes this happens. And dark souls do end their experiences and reconnect to the light.

Remember, simplify life. Simplicity will help you find the light and find the answers.

Look closer into your soul. The future is ending darkness on your world. Healing darkness is easier said than done because fear rules the mind. Add love and light to your mind. No fear of spirits, aliens, or anyone for that matter.

When love finds your world, darkness will release. It's that simple.

What happened to Atlantis is simple. The councils of Atlantis began to call themselves kings of Atlantis. The reptilian mind control became very fearless and destructive. Once the outcasts returned in a friendly manner, they began their mind manipulations—you can say propaganda agents, with lies and deceit and the corruption of the feminine energies.

The women were corrupted first. Due to their own darkness of sexual pleasures, that did lead to reptilian relationships. The positive councils of Atlantis was slowly seduced. Did the Atlanteans begin the first war? Yes, they did. Once the councils were taken over, they felt fear. We will go into more details of this at a later date.

The Atlanteans feared the outcasts of Atlantis and used their abilities to strike first what would later be called Asia Minor. You can say also this was a trap to get the Atlanteans to act on false pretenses. The agenda was to destroy the Atlanteans, and war was the answer.

Only the high councils of Atlantis were manipulated. The citizens of Atlantis had to fend for themselves. The Atlanteans who disagreed with the war and the constant influx of low vibrations fled Atlantis and would later found Egypt.

But first the Atlanteans had to destroy themselves. The modern timeline took over the Earth. As the wars continued with the outcasts and other countries, the high vibrations of Atlantis eroded. The continent became very sexualized and lost. The Lyrans, Pleiadians, and Sirians had no choice but to flee as the Atlanteans savaged the Earth.

The explosions were so fierce the Earth's crust was affected. The outcasts of Atlantis used dirty bombs given to them by the reptilians. Toxic chemicals and also toxic negative beings were attached to these devices, which enforced the lowering of the Atlantean energies.

During these wars Annunaki manipulated the human DNA where the human mind turned into more reptilian. The destruction of humanity was the agenda of the Annunaki and reptilians. Annunaki saw the human threat and potential but also saw them as the perfect slave race. You see this today in your modern culture.

The removal of reptilian mind control almost feels impossible. That's because it seems to be impossible. The human mind has been downgraded to the mind of a rodent. Even a rodent can be very intelligent as an insect slave and the mind of a scavenger and nothing more.

You have the power to remove this hindrance through your thought patterns. You are more than a consumer; you are powerful beings, telepathic humans with telekinesis abilities. And there is so much more–graduating from the third density, not letting mundane problems in the world to control you.

How do you connect to your inner self? Meditation is one way to open your heart. Life is a meditation.

Let yourself go.

Instead of connecting to aliens, connect to yourself and your fellow humans. What happens is during the awakening process. Light workers ignore the third-dimensional humans. They also despise the third-dimensional life.

Realize connecting to your fellow humans, at least the consciousness of third dimension. This is another way to heal your world. The God consciousness lives within everyone. Realize you are God and realize forgiveness is key to healing the foundation of the soul.

If you feel you cannot connect to humans on a personal level, connect to the human consciousness. You might feel as if you are leaving your body. You might feel you have stepped into spirit.

What is happening is that you are connecting to the master timeline, the consciousness timeline where the world is at peace, where the world is put together.

New Human

As you develop your telepathic powers and your mind transitions to the higher dimensions, what is known now will fade away. The third-dimensional life will cease to exist. It will look like a ghost world. The problems and depressions for the third-dimensional world will shift out of existence.

Humans letting go add more love and less worry.

Human consciousness is holding together this current reality–the mainstream media, the politics of your world. The drama of your day will ascend to a higher vibration. A new agenda will occur. Ideas for advanced technologies will come to those who are here to experience it.

A new renaissance will occur, but not one your world has seen before in recorded history. Humans used to the lower dimensions will have trouble ascending. Those holding on to it and who are impatient will get nowhere and will only receive heartache.

To transcend the soul is to give up on worry and connect to what you want to experience. And give it time. The soul must also heal from the third-dimension manipulations. Rest, relax, and experience less stress if possible. Meditation and less angry energies will help you ascend.

Realize also there is nothing to fear.

The soul on a day-to-day basis adds stress, which is called being normal. Releasing that stress will assist with the soul becoming lighter. This is not an easy process but can be connected to gradually.

At this moment the human is limited in its thinking and progress. "You can't do that" is everywhere, isn't it? Unfortunately, jealous is another energy that is known as a block. If I can't do it that means you can't either.

The human consciousness is going into a limitless vibration, meaning you can do anything, but it's up to you.

The Next 1000 Years

The next 1,000 years will bring in the new Earth. Those who connect to aliens, spirits, and angels will experience many hardships but also will lead the awakening. Those who are pressured the hardest will bring in the new world.

Those are selfless will bring in the new Earth.

NASA knows the truth. The truth will set you free if you wish to connect with it. The Earth has several dimensions. Of course they don't teach you this in school. As for a fact, schools are built to look like prisons. It's because they are prisons. There will be a time in the future when most of the Earth's population will awaken to the alien presence.

There will be riots and a connection to beauty. The Earth's frequency will awaken to the higher vibrations. The stressful times will soon vanish as humanity finally accepts the truth. There will be acts of violence but also a romance with love unlike anything seen on this planet–the full circle of the Atlantean experience.

In the beginning the Atlanteans connected to their highest potential but had to fall into darkness to know how to use their power.

You will feel a joy unlike any joy you have ever felt. You will not just see the star people, you will join them, be with them on their ships, rebuild the Earth.

At this moment, humanity is being pushed into its brink and reminded constantly history will repeat itself. But that is not true. New timelines are being built for this new age. The hard truth is that there will not be a third world war. Some individuals are having an issue believing this.

Remember, think simple. Think from the heart. Once you have self-love, you have everything.

Archons

These channeled texts are from spirit guides and higher extraterrestrial beings. We the guides have so much to say. But what is truly causing your planet hostility? Are the Archons in your solar system?

The human belief system can only handle so much. The Archons are one of the most advanced manipulators in the universe. They give the reptilians and Annunaki a run for their money. When you get attacked by a reptilian or negative being, the source of that attack can be from the Archons. Meaning your manipulators are being manipulated by another source.

Archons put the pressure on your planet to learn from it. Master suppressors cannot be reasoned with. To show their power they weaken the mind, so it can be controlled. They do this to the Reptilians also.

Archons can look bat-like, but they have many different appearances and a robotic borg-like form is one of them. Zeta Greys can be similar as for being robotic in nature.

The negative Archons created lower astral. One of the other ways to cut down your world's energy field was to do it astrally. The spirit realm around your planet has been affected tremendously. Wonder why you feel like this is a never winning battle? It's because lower astral is plugged into your planet's consciousness.

This happened in early Atlantean time's. As Atlantis dropped in vibration it dived into lower astral. To give you another understanding, the advanced Atlanteans causing your planet difficulty became Archons. They are currently hitting your planet with everything they got more than ever before.

As your planet becomes more aware of its Atlantean connections, the Archons push even harder against your consciousness. The Atlanteans that destroyed Atlantis became different types of dark beings. Some joined the Illuminati and others became demon energies or Archons. Demon is another word for Archon.

Most of the creatures that you call monsters in your mythology are Archons. Advanced beings that removed the human form and decided to feed off of negative energies. Why do you think these demons look so demonic? Negative human emotions and thoughts created a new species of dark entity.

Your Atlantean times dark entities emerged onto the earth and were seen. The dark entities were another attack on the Atlanteans they could no longer battle. You've seen movies with flying creatures causing anarchy. Those are the Archons.

Your culture of consciousness is allowing this information to come through. As for seeing aliens, the positive and negative has to be understood. Your society does not have an understanding yet. As humanity becomes more curious, you will experience physical connections with these beings.

It's like allowing the movies to come to life. You are in a movie but only experiencing half of its true reality. When souls enter the other side, they see all the beings interacting with humanity. The knowledge doesn't always come at once.

Your planet will experience this also as it ascends to the 4th dimension. The more the soul becomes ready to see what is happening on your planet, the closer you will be to interacting with the physical realities you are reaching out to.

We must conclude this message.

We will continue later.

Jesus and Atlantis

Jesus was an Atlantean, from its humble beginnings to its ending defeat. At the end of Atlantean wars Jesus was not a positive soul. He had lost his way like most Atlanteans, but his agenda was very different from the others.

He wanted to explore the darkness of humanity by becoming part of it, to later uplift it from its amnesia. He sought to find the devil within his soul and show the earth his wrath. There was much dark sorcery and Jesus was one of these sorcerers. He did not die after Atlantis was destroyed. He went to Egypt and caused more havoc.

Bringing his power to Egypt imbued spiritual significance into the land. He was later destroyed by more advanced beings. He used the oceans to protect him, while on land, he was weaker with his abilities. He would later advance his power for the greater good.

Yes, Jesus and other Atlanteans had the ability to fly. Even with their dark ways, the sorcerers of Atlantis were able to manipulate the energies of the earth to visit the skies, to show the weaker Atlanteans that the way of dark was all there was.

The dark sorcerers of Atlantis were worshiped by their followers. The wicked Jesus was all powerful but also inspired the abilities of other Atlanteans. If there was a dark power, there must be a light power also.

As the Atlanteans lowered their vibrations, they lost information over time. It was no longer easy to connect to all known knowledge. The sorcerers of Atlantis that were connected to the hall of records to sustain their abilities. But even they were weaker than their ancestors.

When Jesus arrived, he was born into a wealthy aristocratic, Jewish family of Atlantis. At this time there were many races of Atlanteans, including those with blue skin, yellow skin, and several others that no longer exist.

The Ancient Atlanteans were also Arabic. Being born into negative sorcery is like being born into a family of bankers. Modern time bankers are very wise with mind control. Money is a seducer that they control very well and they manage the minds of the many.

As Jesus aged, his powers were known very well. Mind control was his favorite. As for a healing, he never utilized that talent. You could say that Jesus was the Merlin of his time. Demonic energies were well-known to him. His path wasn't just for destruction. Like a Reptilian being, he carried the force to show humanity's potential.

Sacred sites around the world have Jesus' energies.

Lumerians are known to fly also. Not all of them utilized those talents but many did explore them. Atlanteans would visit the Lumerians to heal after a great war. Some Lumerians were captured and forced into healing.

One of the reasons mermaids look human is because they had sexual encounters and had children. The ancient mermaids appeared very alien to your world and most were Sirian.

Many Sirians became frustrated with the human race after their species was experimented on and savaged by war. Some Sirians came back to earth reincarnated into wealth.

During this time, King Solomon was one of the sorcerers of Atlantis as well.

Jesus and King Solomon fought each other and became mortal enemies. Too add more understanding, Jesus at this time was a fallen angel reincarnated as human, exploring the darkness of the realms before his Earth incarnation.

Jesus and King Solomon have been brothers in past lives on other worlds.

The path for earth was to awaken it. But first it was shut down from spirit.

The Atlanteans were like children. Very advanced, but they needed soul expansion to further explore the human condition. The Atlanteans had to shut down their higher knowledge. During this time, the Atlanteans had large amounts of knowledge. But, to further explore the human experience, the higher knowledge had to be erased.

The Annunaki turning humans into a slave race and in many ways went too far but not necessary. The reasons humans are so lost is because they are cut off almost completely from the akashic records.

The modern human is part of a mass hypnosis under an Archon mind control. Losing all knowledge was a gift. Worldwide amnesia took over the planet after Atlantis was destroyed. Other worlds have been through the same.

The Planet Maldek went through the same. But when they lost their higher knowledge, their planet was destroyed. To lose higher consciousness knowledge requires courage and bravery amd not many civilizations survive.

The human race on earth would have been destroyed centuries ago, if it wasn't for the DNA and the human spirit that evolved within the human consciousness. This planet has found gold. That gold is within each human on the planet. Humanity is currently reactivating its Atlantean ways. And the journey to higher knowledge will not be easy.

But don't give up.

The future will have no wars. Humanity will reunite. The cycle of the third dimension has finished its course. Be strong and continue with your journey. This isn't for nothing.

The puzzle pieces of your fourth dimension are coming together.

Your connection to aliens will increase. Most importantly, the amnesia will end. Realize that having amnesia on a planet like this is one of the hardest experiences one soul can endure. Realize also that these written connections will continue. We in the spirit world will continue to give you information until your planet reaches the fifth dimension.

At that point, you will be moving the spirit world into other dimensions and will add your libraries of knowledge to trillions of worlds. This journey is a hard one but worth it.

Syria Channeling
Law of One 4-14-18

What is happening with Syria? Assad, the President of Syria, is not the problem. He is not perfect, but the global elite wants him out. He is helping the Syrian people, but his efforts are not always going to be recognized.

Syria's location is near many stargates and alien portal energies. Many negative Sirian races are using Syria to lower humanities consciousness. It's not always the reptilians causing difficulties; not to say reptilians are not involved. But this is a Sirian controversy.

Realise aliens see the future. Syria is one of the last places of conflict that can be fully ruled. Iraq still plays a part in the global manipulation, but Syria is the hot spot. Iran can't be taken over and much of the deep state are getting desperate.

Realize that those of you who do not want war are always going to be manipulated until you raise your vibration to the 4th dimension. Raise your consciousness and you see your aliens.

The Sirians are connected to Saudi Arabia, and they do not always play nice with the deep state. They have no trouble selling out the Saudis that they made rich. The alien Sirians helped the House of Saud become rich and powerful.

In ancient times, the Sirians quietly invaded the Arab world, using wealth as a way to convince the royal families to give in to the Sirian agenda. Mecca is the capital of the manipulation over Saudi Arabia and Syria. The United Arab Emirates is under this control, also. Over the years, the manipulation has eased – but not entirely.

Mecca is what is controlling the leaders of the Arab world. Sirian councils, called the Quan, come from Sirius B. Their agenda is not positive. Some of these Sirians are reptilian in appearance. Their manipulations extend to Egypt.

Quan were refugees from Orion that were forced to leave Sirius B after manipulating its councils and taking many Sirian women hostage. The woman were transformed into men and used as leaders.

When Quan found Earth, it was easy prey. For years, they settled in the desert regions of Saudi Arabia, not to be seen, figuring out their next plan and laying low as they were being tracked by the Law of One.

The Law of One is a positive Sirian Council that resides on Earth at this time. They connect to the Galactic Federation of Light watching over the Earth's oceans. The Pacific and the Atlantic ocean can be as dense as the desert regions of your world. Many alien star bases are under water, deep within the Pacific Rim.

If you ever see an alien spacecraft near the ocean, it will most likely be in the Pacific. The area is open and there is less traffic than the Atlantic. More Reptilian and Zeta bases are within the depths of the Atlantic Ocean.

Not to say all are malevolent.

The Law of One has always been connected to Egypt and Atlantis. They never interfered with the human experience; but as Quan became an influence, it was too late to turn the manipulation around. Quan and the Annunaki took over the Arab world, with Mecca being the capital of manipulation.

The idea was to lose the women and let the men rule the world. Women would reject the manipulations, so they had to be seen as evil. Quan told the males to destroy the females and to use them only for reproduction and the home – nothing more.

The negative reptilians had their moments of darkness, but the Sirians took it a step further – to do away with the females all together, and even have the males reproduce all on their own. Experiments were conducted for men to have children, and these hybrids were destroyed after many failures.

The Law of One interfered by destroying these test sites. Some of the illuminati carry these traits currently. Male hybrid humans were created to have children. This is a common Sirian trait within the alien species. A good portion of the species carries these traits.

Wonder why there are so many females in the workforce, with no children, who have lazy husbands or partners? Within some Lyran feline races, the males birth the children and care for the home. Sirians, Pleiadians, Orions and Andromedans have worlds like this.

Your planet is more reptilian, so the roles are switched, with the female being the mother and caretaker. To be close to and bond with the children, many females take on the birthing role. Without that bond, mothers feel very alone and isolated. Being a boss at work and having no family at home is very lonely. So, many females take on the birthing role to have that connection to their children.

Some mothers never connect to their children on your world. Some believe just having a child will open the maternal instinct and that doesn't always happen.

Back to discussing Quan.

The malevolent Sirians are always battling the malevolent Reptilians, changing timelines that cause humans to feel ill. When a human gets sick out of nowhere, most likely a timeline was just shifted. Timeline shifts can also conflict with the weather. The wars in earth's past can be connected to timeline wars – Galactic wars on other star systems.

To tell you the truth, right now, the reason why most humans will not acknowledge aliens on your planet is because they want no part of it – because most of the humans on your world have had enough of it. When you connect to the negative energies of a world like this, you pull in negative memories with aliens, such as fear.

This is simple – but also complicated.

We will continue with the Sirian and Reptilian connections in the next chapter.

Mecca

The feline Lyrans have been protecting earth for billions of years. There were many incidents aimed to destroy earth. The Reptilians wanted earth for themselves – the dinosaur experiment was not working. Earth was intended by the Reptilians to be a dinosaur world, and having humans and dinosaurs roam the earth together was the plan...

As long as the reptilians ruled the planet.

The Sirian councils decided for a human experience on this planet – a planet for everyone. The human experiment was to continue on earth. The positive Reptilians integrated with Ashtar Command to assist with Earth's protection and have the negative Reptilians removed from earth. If the Reptilians could not have it, Earth was going to be destroyed. Many lessons were learned from Lyra. The many defenses around earth increased. The wars between the Reptilians and the Lyrans caused the dinosaurs to be extinct.

The modern earth human was being created through alien technology. The modern human was a mix of the alien species visiting the planet at the time. The modern human went through many versions, with the first humans being very advanced and evil, while the Neanderthal human was developed and left alone to evolve.

This new version of human was denser, and complicated in ways never seen before. They had characteristics that were not seen for some time in the most advanced beings. Tribal humans were very primitive and intense with rage, with ape and Reptilian traits being very obvious.

Humans with both ape and Reptilian DNA had an energy that clashed. As a Neanderthal, the human was calm at a third dimensional form and a primitive energy that would go out of control with rage, but for the most part, a humble being.

As the DNA was enhanced with the primate humans, many different kinds of beings evolved. The Sasquatch and Dodman also came from these early experiments. Different versions of the Sasquatch were invented through out time as the human evolved.

34

Mecca came to be the center of the earth. The foundation of what the world should follow. The current agenda was to control the mind. Culture is another word for mind control in your world.

During the middle ages, magic was everywhere and never truly understood. Over time, magic went underground. Now, the elite rule magic on your planet. Modern day slavery is linked to commerce. The modern consumer is the modern slave, fitting into the modern mix of mind control to be recognized and be successful.

The gods that once ruled your planet have turned into modern day money, religion and consumerism. The modern controllers are quiet these days, using celebrity and power to set future agendas.

The modern human is told not to believe that these manipulative forces are here – to go with the flow, make a living, be complacent, and, most of all, accept the reality told to you that aliens are not here on this planet in another dimension. To play the part of ordinary humans. Don't forget -you have no power.

The myths are nothing else. They are just myths. The modern generation knows better and all is well in the world. Humans are not to realize there are higher dimensional beings here helping humanity. But there are others who want to keep humanity as mind controlled slaves.

Black magic is used everyday, never mentioned in modern conversations with the masses. Humans are not to know that modern magic is being used to manipulate the minds of the masses. Mecca is a mind control center, and so is Washington, DC. Currently, London is silent and so is the Vatican. But look at America, which is always in world news conversations.

Modern Rome is setting the agenda for earth. Mecca has much of the illuminati members upgrading their powers by draining the energies of humanity. The illuminati black magicians are not to be seen by the modern human. Mecca is one of the sources of their power.

The Vatican is a place for rituals. There are many sacred sites connected to the druids, which the illuminati mind also control and to keep their magic seducing humanity. Modern religion gives power to the illuminati. The more you worship to man created gods, such as the Pope, the more you give your power to the elite.

There is nothing wrong with worshiping god. Realize this: worshiping Buddha or Jesus gives the elite power. You have the freedom to do as you wish. The elite manipulate the energies of the earth. Following the guidelines of a simple holiday gives the elite power. And even a wedding can give them power, because the elite are there to control your marriage. This isn't always the case. But realize religion is normally pulled into marriage in the ceremony. You can be married to the illuminati, also. Married to their agenda.

Messages From the Outer World

Egypt is your ancient Atlantis. The Egyptian energies have been alive long before your earth was created, and is known by many different names. Orion is their source energy and most of you will recognize that.

Notice the different hieroglyphs and see how many different species of aliens that visited your world. And realize your planet is safe. There are many challenges ahead, and you know this. The energy circles of Orion surround your planet to keep it safe. It is true humans decide who comes to this world and who does not.

You, as Earth humans, control your reality. If you wish for a positive alien visitation, you will have it. It's up to your human collective to know us and understand our intentions. Many fear us, so that is one of the reasons for our visitations to be far from being realized.

Humanity has not decided on a whole if they want us to connect to your race – us being the Orions, the Yahyels and the Zetas collectives. The wisdom of your planet is still keeping us at a distance, as there is so much healing needed for your world – poverty and abusive connections with family and personal love relationships.

We are not that hard to reach. So much fear has been embedded on your planet's consciousness. Any idea or connection to extraterrestrial life is almost forbidden entirely in your world. We brought you languages and technologies and watched you grow. We have been watching you grow from the beginning of time. We are not your fathers. We are your friends and family.

The idea is to find your inner happiness. Find your inner soul that speaks out often but is often ignored due to belief systems. The soul energies of this planet are connected to the Arcturian collective consciousness.

The Arcturians, with permission, can hear your thoughts and be a part of your soul mission. Every human on your planet visits an Arcturian reality during your incarnation on planet Earth – a school of the higher soul, you can say. During great challenges, many of you connect to the Arcturians and visit their healing chambers in astral. You can disconnect to your soul-being and lose yourself entirely through grief. It's always your choice what direction you go in life.

Many lower astral beings use grief and suffering as a way to convince the soul they are victims. There is no hope. There is nothing to live for...when, in fact, you have everything to live for. But it's always your choice to choose your direction. Challenges are to uplift you and even take you to another direction. Conflict is not there to discourage you from following your soul desire. Conflict is there to open you up. That's why there are so many conflicts on your planet. The soul wishes to grow, and it's how you use that growth that is up to you. All conflict has a purpose to advance the soul experience.

Suicide takes the soul into the unknown. The soul chooses what conflict to experience. The more you connect to the light during a suicide experience, the quicker you will heal. Realize that the soul will lose fragmentation and split apart. Other versions of the soul will be scattered and you will feel this intensity. Healing from a suicide is never a simple matter. As the fragments of the soul scatter, they get manipulated, and healing those manipulations can take years or decades. You can pass into the gates of heaven. But those fragments are lost and reconnecting to them is never easy. Realize those fragments can be used for darkness.

Souls that have experienced suicide usually take the effects of the suicide into future incarnations. Realize contracts were broken and now you are living a new incarnation. Usually reconnecting to a new incarnation is not easy to continue a new contract – meaning there are souls that continue the suicide process. Depending on the soul, it will take five incarnations to break the cycle. Realize the soul is normally tortured by the past suicide energies.

The soul has the choice to continue a lifetime. You can break the suicide cycle.

Where is Atlantis and the Illuminati?

The Illuminati took over the Atlantean energies, took over their influence over the world. The Greek architecture is very Atlantean.

The temples of Greece were once Atlantean temples. The architecture style lives on as you can see with the Roman empire. So the Atlantean influence still exists. The Parthenon in Athens is a perfect example of Atlantean influence. Once an Atlantean temple, it was converted to the Greek culture of the day.

Not all temples of Greece are Atlantean, but you see the influence. Rome wanted that world dominance and did not realize they were connecting to ancient Atlantis.

With the destruction of Atlantis, what did live beyond them was their religious powers. It wasn't a religion, but it might as well have been—powerful psychic powers and telekinetic energies almost beyond other alien races.

To sum it up, Atlanteans could not handle the power as you have most likely heard from other sources. It's like giving a newborn baby a high-powered sports car, a primitive race with advanced abilities but not enough maturity to handle its power.

If you need a simplified understanding of the Atlanteans, they are still here today in secret. Some joined the Illuminati and continued the manipulations. Others became wizards of your world, which eventually became the religions of your planet. Aliens Zeus and the Egyptian gods lost their way as humans became easy to manipulate.

Once the guardians of hope started to enslave humanity. Never saw this before, so you can say this is an experimentwatching a race of people more than willing to enslave society was unheard of.

There are sale worlds in the universe. The Earth human volunteers to be a slave race. You see this today as slavery is seen as modern-day life. Modern slavery is called culture in your world.

Atlantis lives within modern religion. Its power still reigns in your world. The magic is used for slavery of the mind. During the last years of Atlantis, the people thought they were doing the right thing, fighting other continents for reasons unknown, fictional reasons that would lead into your current timelines as for meaningless wars. Manufactured by manipulations became comprehension.

Many of your politicians are ancient Atlanteans continuing their manipulations. Thomas Jefferson was an ancient Atlantean politician, a sorcerer with great influence. Your modern world is an echo of the past.

The magic of ancient Babylon was Atlantean. The Babylonian world is your current world. The symbols and manipulations are a constant.

It is also highly likely your aliens will begin to interact with humans again. Don't forget they know your race very well. Deception is seen a mile away. Even before the deception is created, they see it coming.

As of this writing, in the next ten years, you should begin to see more alien activity on your planet. This can change due to human reaction. They can easily change their minds and give you a few hundred years to sort out your issues with each other.

The Atlantean energies are everywhere. You can find their magic in religious places of your planet. Remove the manipulations and you will feel the Atlantean energies. The Archons use the Atlantean energies to fool humans, take your power away by saying you have no power.

The average thought pattern of a human is that humans are powerless, farthest from the truth.

As for your Illuminati and their location, follow the money and you will find them. The largest corporations have their symbols and influence. Look at your Fortune 500 and also the richest families in the world.

The thirteen families you are familiar with, but it goes much deeper. Lockheed Martin and General Dynamics is an Illuminati front. Boeing is turning more to the positive but not completely. These giant companies are here to build vortexes and tell you what to think.

Also they are here building the matrix you live in. The large tech companies are the overlords of your matrix. How many own a phone or a TV? Just look at the influence of that device. And also the media on those devices are a company from the same force that created them.

How would you feel if it was one company running your planet? You would freak out, correct? That's the bad guy. So the companies are all separate but continuing the same agenda. Babylon is now a corporation continuing the same rituals to control your reality.

Google and Boeing are split as for corruption of manipulation, meaning they haven't been fully taken over. Boeing is coming out of its manipulation after decades of control. As for Raytheon, that's another story. If you want a public company that is connected to the Illuminati, it's Raytheon.

Mind control operations and chemtrail technologies just to name a few agendas. All these top defense corporations also work with the black projects. In secret they continue the agenda. For the most part, the public sectors of these companies have no idea. But executives at the top are CIA and other intelligence agencies.

Cut these companies in half. The public front is for the shareholders and millionaires to be made, using out-of-this-world technologies for a war that will never happen. Enough weapons to destroy the planet, and how is it our society seems like it's stuck in the Stone Age.

Society warfare with racism and corruption politics is all there to keep the children at a low vibration. Money is to keep humanity at a low vibration. Money is not just control, it's there to manipulate the energies of human consciousness.

The consciousness is to stall and not grow spiritually. It's difficult to do so when you are worried about feeding yourself, worried where the next paycheck is coming from. It's all done by design.

Atlantis is still here; you just have to find it. The reactivation of humanity will bring Atlantis back into the physical reality. At the moment, most of Atlantis is in fourth dimension–at least what is left of it.

You can say the aliens in the fourth dimension are in the Atlantis dimension.

What is lifting now is the Archon Dimension or Archon Grid that is surrounding your planet. As the human consciousness continues to rise, the truth will find you. Believing in yourselves is the major key. Believing in your higher dimensional self will open the higher vibrations just as you imagine it.

There are dark Atlanteans using their spells on the human consciousness. They don't like to be seen, but they are very real. Humans have been downgraded to an animal-like vibration. Wake up, get dressed, and go to work.

When the higher shifts awaken within you, humanity will no longer need sleep or a shower. You will always be awake. Some will look for rest. Most will want to stay awake to explore and continue the human experience.

As you awaken you will connect to the Illuminati forces, those of positive and negative. When upgrading your vibrations, you will see light and dark much differently. The benefits of both will be more clear.

The Archon vortex lives within the mind at the moment. It's hard to think, and yes, the Annunaki are involved also. Humans are known to punish themselves and each other. That must come to an end.

The Quran

Realize happiness can be found within. The fourth dimension is with you, and the higher dimensions aren't too far away. As religion was brought to your world, the higher dimensions of your world slowly vanished.

To go further, religion connects to the lower dimensions of worlds that wish to hold your planet captive. The Quran was to unite humanity in the Middle East but instead divided it. The alien text was manipulated, and the consciousness of earth was hijacked.

The Sirians brought a gift to earth. That gift was alien knowledge. This knowledge was weaponized and used against humanity by the reptilians, mostly by the draconians. The architecture of manipulation connected to the root chakra and poisoned it. All the chakras were poisoned with violence.

This is why healing the chakras is so important–reconnecting to the universe and finding your galactic families once again, reaching to the vortex of your founders. The chakras represent worlds you come from. Sirius, Venus, and even the sun is connected to you.

The giants of the past were erased because they showed how alien your planet truly was. To get humans to murder each other was the master plan. The Quran played a large part in it, as the Quran has many Atlantean secrets from the high priests. The text was to reactivate the soul. Instead the Quran poisons the soul with violence.

The draconian way is to hold the mind and control the thoughts and actions that will lead to violence because violence holds the earth in the third dimension. But there is so much more because the Quran was to be a text of peace and a galactic bible for the third dimension, to unite humanity, and instead the divide is immense. There is a family energy around the Quran. Unfortunately that energy has been poisoned for many centuries.

As we continue with this religious subject, we want to mention the pope, who is always a weak soul and sometimes with a heart but usually a human that is easily manipulated. A weak soul is needed to compromise the people into submission.

A strong pope would speak out and destroy the Catholic Church. Weakness is needed even if strength is hinted at. That strength is manipulated to serve the Draconian agenda.

41

The mind of the Archons is simple. Let good be brought to the earth. Later on we will manipulate it, find its weakness, and slowly alter the energies to serve our higher purpose.

Why do the Archons have so much power over earth? It is because humanity in the ancient times surrendered. The wars in the past was a past against the Archons, and to erase the ideas of alien connections with your planet.

Why do so many humans not believe in the alien forces around your planet? Weakness in the consciousness made it normal to feel humans are alone in the universe.

The bloodshed of the past gave humanity no choice but to surrender because the souls that kept the earth safe were no more. They were destroyed and removed from the planet. Those speaking about aliens now are those that fought the wars on your battlefield.

Realize also comfort in the third dimension made it easy to forget the alien presence on your planet—a nice life living well and a vacation for two on the Bahamas.

The wars of the past were humans fighting aliens. History made sure that knowledge was forgotten.

The war of manipulation continues until humanity awakens from its slumber. The astral world has been constantly reaching out to your dimension and is easily forgotten, seen in fiction only as the prison planet continues to ignore the energies around you.

The Quran was the break of humanity from the fifth dimension. These religious texts were built to take humanity down and imprison it. The rape and murder on your planet must be healed before it goes fully into the fifth dimension.

Love is all.

The Quran On Other Worlds

Understand other worlds influence planet earth: Venus, Mercury, Saturn, and other worlds in other star systems. The secret governments know this because they visit these places on a daily basis. That's their reality while humanity is on one planet. The elite travel to other worlds in secret, in other dimensions. Children are abducted and brought to other worlds, mainly Mars. The technique is very simple using technology and the knowledge that you are doing the right thing. Humanity needs to be enslaved. It's the right thing to do, so we can have all the power and do as we do. Live free as the weak suffer on earth. The Quran shows the weakness in man as humanity uses violence towards each other. The same thought pattern is used by the elite, as the Quran opens portals to other worlds. Violent acts allow dark entities to travel through your world freely. The new education system will be about spirituality on a galactic scale.

In Sirius there is a world called Bruce. This is a world of the elite one of them at least. Once a barren planet, but now it's full of life. Paradise world, where the elite live in luxury in the fourth dimension. You can call it a forbidden zone, and understand the name of the planet is to keep it simple. Think of this as a Garden of Eden for the elite, and many of the elite aren't even human. Many are feline and dragon-like in appearance in a human form, but they aren't called human. Felines that can change color with a single thought. Normally this planet is left alone, meaning other Sirians keep their distance, and it's not also easy to find either as it is very close to Sirius C. To give you another understanding of the elite or illuminati, many are in human form but deformed as for face structure and even body structure. Their mental powers are intense, but their looks can be hideous.

The Martians' elite is who we are describing at this time. They were persecuted in the past for their appearance, another reason for the monks of your past hiding their appearance behind a hooded cloak. Ever heard of a powerful monk? The elite are hidden, and the cloak was invented for them to disappear. The time of ancient Atlantis, the reptilians pressured the Atlanteans to go against the Martians because of their appearance. Alien wars are constant on your planet. Your mythology is a sign of the past alien connections. As you reactivate you will understand this. The deactivated human is currently on your planet in the billions. Annunaki money plagues the consciousness to control the thoughts of humanity. Money has been weaponized and is used to divide everyone. A Sirian creation is used as a gift and only a gift.

Planet Clear is another world the Quran is connected to, deep within Sirius and a hidden star system called the forbidden zone. This is an Annunaki planet where the elite are connected also, a battle planet that can look similar to Egypt, a desert planet with Egyptian like architecture throughout the world. This is a slave planet. Humans are brought here to reproduce and be configured into this reality, meaning they have no idea earth even exists. To help you understand, many that come from the planet Clear are now reincarnated on your world as sex slaves and are known for sexual services such as prostitution and strip clubs. The pimps used to be Annunaki from the planet Clear. There's a great amount of richness to this planet with diamond luxury, a beautiful slave planet in the desert. Dubai has a lot of similarities, Kazakhstan and Saudi Arabia to name a few others. Disease doesn't really exist on this planet. So when souls incarnate on your world from Clear, they easily fall prey to disease. Sexual pleasures are a plus on planet Clear. Unfortunately no one has any rights and you can be taken or abducted by the powerful without a problem. If you fight back you die. So the rich cities in the Arab world are connected to planet Clear. The portals and vortexes are connected to Clear. You must be careful because once again, your rights mean nothing. Once the elite want you, it's over. Those that wear the gold are the powerful. Anyone else wearing gold will be destroyed. Basically humans are indoctrinated into thinking a certain way. Sounds familiar? Some are micro chipped and some are not. There is no money system just a control system. Follow the rules and you will be fine. Also Lucifer's energy surrounds planet Clear.

Many citizens of your world reincarnated from a slave planet. Souls go from slave planet to slave planet because of the teachings they learn. When the world goes into higher vibration, they just leave. There are souls that are underdeveloped and need the third-dimension energies to grow. How are they at such a low vibration? The curiosity of a dense environment. The physical world can be an addiction. Some incarnate in the physical, but that is what they prefer and will do anything to keep it that way.

Earth is graduating to the fourth and fifth dimensions and even higher. The population will decrease because of this. Scholars will stay and be with the world until it achieves its highest vibration. The scholars are those assisting earth to achieve its high vibration. And they are currently incarnated on earth at this time. The path to the fourth dimension will not be easy. The slaves of the third dimension are used to being slaves. Unlocking from the third will feel like it's impossible. It's like losing one's identity. How will the fourth dimension affect earth? The surrounding energies will change such as the way of life. How you live life will change. Same as any new era enters into the new generations. What was once old will be forgotten. Where humans used to walk they will fly. A less dense earth–humans will feel more angelic and more telepathic. Energies will glow around you. Astral travel will simplify itself and be easier for all of you. Heal the slave mentality on your planet. It is called normal, but in truth it is not as you know.

Saturn

Saturn is the forbidden planet and is still active with a civilization. It is also known as the lost world, and once again there is life on this planet at a higher dimension. Reptilian influence moved into this planet long ago.

When you look at illuminati symbolism, Saturn is mentioned many times. The lost world could not make a decision of what side it should be on so it's very divided. Same as Earth but Saturn is at a higher dimension.

The positive beings aren't always to be seen by all aliens. Normally the higher dimension of Saturn is fifth dimension. The lower vibrations are at fourth dimension. But that does not mean fifth dimension can't be infiltrated by lower-vibration beings.

A war in space and Saturn was involved with it. Mars usually gets the bad rap of being the god of war. In this channeling we are here to tell you, Saturn is far worse. Most Saturn beings are in human form but not exactly as humans.

Many are skinny with five fingers and no reason to have food. Energy is food; different vibrations are considered food. There are mountains and springs where your energies can be recharged. Saturn beings appear as gas-like beings and can take a more physical form if they must.

As they pass through the different dimensions that is known as long-distance travel, where a single thought takes them there, what they are missing is emotions. There are known to be intense beings of the light and dark.

They have emotions but not as intense as the humans on earth. It's more direction and sometimes is hostile. Most of the dimensions are interchangeable, meaning they're always in movement and you are never in the same place every day. You are always somewhere new.

They don't have homes. The entire planet is a home.

When earth came into existence Saturn invaded. You can say earth was pulled towards this current solar system to be imprisoned by it. The architecture of earth was very different, and you can say earth was a playground everyone wanted.

The beings of Saturn can be worse than the Archons because Saturn can be more destructive. If we can't have it we will destroy it. And Saturn infiltrated the reptilians that were guarding earth, the positive reptilians. Saturn beings are known for possession and can look demonic in third dimension.

Saturn's energies can be found in the Jinn. You can see the Jinn is the new god of earth that wishes to be worshiped. Understanding the dark entities of your planet will assist will freeing the manipulations.

Lower astral was brought onto earth's surface and hidden in the third dimension. Horror movies and kind of negative thought gives power to lower astral. Negative actions strengthen lower astral to remain on the third-dimension level.

Lower astral is like a mask over humanity. Children see these dark entities as soon as they are born. They see angels also, but of course, the dark ones are welcomed on the earth's surface and rule the human consciousness.

To give you more insight, Saturn is another world where the illuminati exist. This is the planet where they live. They don't control the entire planet but most of it. Once again there is a divide between positive and negative on this world. Saturn has not healed the divide, but earth is giving the divide power.

When the earth heals, Saturn will heal also.

Saturn is the home of Satan and, unfortunately, father of earth, with the same influence as Mars. Saturn rules the male human on earth and even the female. Understand during the development process of a child, the mother and the child are cursed by Saturn and Mars. It goes much further with other alien entities, but in this text we will speak of Mars and Saturn.

Saturn wants the development of the child to be as difficult as possible. You are not allowed on earth to enter the forbidden planet because you also entering the forbidden solar system. You are being marked and even cursed for being here.

The curse is the mental curse of negativity. A mental frown is implanted on the child and mother. Realize this can be healed, but it's not always easy to heal. The mental frown is depression. The Martian wants the female off the planet for good.

The female was cursed for staying on earth. The Pleiadians and Lyrans wouldn't allow the female to be removed from earth. The Sirian at one time threatened to destroy Saturn. After earth was plagued by Saturn's manipulation. It was impossible.

When humans incarnate on earth, many souls travel through Saturn. This is another entry point as there are many. Many deceptive beings incarnate through Saturn such as Aleister Crowley and many of the Satanists of your world. The Bush family is another one.

Martin Luther King, Jr. was incarnated through Saturn and also Elvis. For better and for worse, Julius Caesar was incarnated through Saturn also.

To explain further, there are many entry points into earth such as Agartha and Sirius, the Pleiades, Arcturus, and Andromeda just to name a few. They all have entry points into the astral plane surrounding earth.

The fastest way to incarnate on earth is through lower astral.

In the past, Agartha was the earth. Elemental beings such as elves, fairies, dragons, and other higher dimensional beings were the true earth. Elementals from Sirius and the Pleiadians inhabited the planet long before the manipulation began.

These beings were always seen by lower vibrations such as the reptilians and insectoids. To go even further, the earth was created in another dimension, the Grey Dimension which was in another universe, the Grey universe, but earth was a spark of light.

In its early days, it was already surrounded by darkness. The Grey Dimension is an Archon universe. The earth at that time was separate from the Grey Dimension. Even in the very beginning the planet was under siege.

To be clear, this wasn't an Archon planet.

Many wars covered the earth's surface. Alien life gave further birth to earth's nature. Mother Earth herself is nature, a nature being of trees and planets. Earth is called a seed planet. Mother Earth is a seed being.

She can turn a moon into a planet, making it a life force.

Life on Saturn

The illuminati, both positive and negative, live on Saturn. This is the spiritual world that watches everything. Mars has the military operations and is mostly remembered in astral. All the planets in your solar system have life in other dimensions.

The gas beings on Saturn can be very vicious to unwanted visitors. These beings can be seen in the third dimension. Basically you are not welcomed here.

The positive illuminati is making peace with earth at this time.

To describe the positive illuminati–they were angelic in energy, a world of light, and you can say the archangels are part of this group–Pleiadians, Sirians, Arcturians, Lyrans, and Andredians. Realize this is the aliens' aspect of the illuminati. Requirement is a human lifetime that is heavily enlisted with lessons.

Basically you must incarnate within the pyramid of the illuminati and make your choice of which side you wish to be on. To be in this elite group is to incarnate within the illuminati timeline, which is different than the human timeline.

They are very connected to spirit and never truly let go unless they wish to leave.

We want you to know there are different kinds of illuminati. There is third dimension, fourth dimension, and fifth dimension illuminati energies.

The third dimension is your Rothschild and Rockefellers and so on. They like to keep a low profile and deny everything. From time to time, they like to share their power and influence, such as world domination and a population reduction.

Look at it this way when the illuminati says population reduction. The consciousness increases its population, even too much of a population, just to shut down those plans.

The fourth dimension illuminati is Pleiadian, Sirian, Annunaki, Martian influences. Positive and negative live within these groups, and these groups are very small. They do talk to each other, and you can say it's a game of strategy.

To give you another perspective, the serpent reptilian is at the top of the pyramid. The serpent isn't usually spoken about too often as aggressive. As usual, there are positive and negative, and anytime you see serpents in movies and literature, they are showing their presence.

To add to your research into the higher dimensions, the negative illuminati did lose during the renaissance period. Over time they did regain control, but the dark forces did lose their influence. Notice the Greek knowledge that resurfaced such as technology. Leonardo da Vinci and his influence were kept secret because people did not understand during that time period.

Leonardo da Vinci was a Greek inventor in the past also. Familiar energies were brought forward once again. To go into it further, Leonardo was assisting Jules Verne in astral to be comfortable connecting to flight and submarine technologies.

Now for the fifth dimension illuminati.

Cartoons that connect to the astral plane are here to help humanity adapt to the higher dimensions. Once the fifth and sixth dimensions begin, they further influence your planet. The universe is speaking to you.

The fifth dimension can influence war and peace very easily. They can destroy your planet without hesitation. There are several reasons your planet still exists. The largest reason is that humanity wants a chance to show the universe they can raise to the higher dimensions. They want a chance, and they failed many times in the past.

You will not fail this time.

The human consciousness on earth does not want to be destroyed. Humanity asked for alien assistance because at the third dimension it's not so easy to fix the higher dimensional problems. The main message here is that you are saving yourself.

Some channelings look at humans as foolish, and that is true. But so is everyone at a low vibration with an Archon influence. That doesn't not mean you don't know what you are doing. Think of negativity as a pizza buffet.

Humanity is eating a lot of pizza. Look at pizza as knowledge. Humanity can't get enough of the third dimensional knowledge. So you call in the aliens to help you on your journey.

Are you children? Yes and no to that question.

Humanity is absorbing third dimension at a massive rate. Almost like a crack addict with an unlimited amount of drugs. You need help with your addiction. This is a good addiction, but it can get out of hand.

At the third dimension, it's hard to know when to stop or to slow down and smell the roses of the higher dimensions.

Life on Saturn.

The Rothschild energies come from Saturn. The influence and manipulation goes hand in hand. Realize during the centuries, this manipulation has been many names. The Saturn manipulation takes on Roman families that are of influence throughout the centuries.

Taking a third dimensional form. The Roman illuminati isn't mentioned much or at all. The ancient Greek illuminati was destroyed once the Roman influence increased.

Illuminati influences began in Atlantis.

The influence entered Babylon, Suminaria, Egypt, Greece, and Rome.

The major influence of illuminati is Roman. Notice the location of the Vatican. Humans with no name you can call them, dark magicians that influenced and destroyed Merlin. They used Merlin to create an empire, and he fought against them.

The English rule could have been more powerful. Merlin removed his influence and went into hiding, which also destroyed the King Arthur influence. Arthur was erased from history for a reason. When the myth was discovered and manipulated, it continued its dark turn over the royal families.

Magic was intended to influence your reality in the public. But instead, it was buried. It was intended to have a dark magician as a king of your royal family. King Arthur was to be that king to start it off. He was too weak and influenced by darkness.

Magic still continues, but now it is hidden. Arthur was to be a positive influence. The pressure of power was too much, and he cracked, taking his empire down with him. Spiritual sorcery was to continue throughout the ages. Instead it was hidden as it is today.

To go further, the illuminati is on all planets, including yours. They don't call themselves this or use a label. The architects of reality is what they truly are.

Humanity connects to timelines of creation and creates a reality. The architects lay down the foundation, and humanity chooses if they wish to experience it or not. Those who reject the program either change timelines or move to another country or town. The other alternative is to wait until an exit point comes through.

Timelines are always shifting through reality. The majority want it there, and so it exists. Saturn gives it power such as the other worlds to continue its teachings. The lessons rejected from Saturn are used on earth all the time. Basically if you don't want slavery, earth will take it.

High vibrational worlds won't accept murder as an experience. Earth will accept the murder experience and quadruple it. Instead of a few murders a day, earth will have thousands.

On Saturn Archons take another form. They bullied Saturn with their treatments working and not working, such as society and how it conducted itself. Life on Saturn was not easy in the past. What was rejected found a home on earth.

The structure of conflict with the soul redefining itself–meaning when you incarnate on a world, you can change drastically when that life chooses its exit. Most worlds do not have this, and Saturn experimented with it.

Enough tension to break the soul, break it away from its old ways, a shift more drastic than most planets. Earth seems to be the perfect place for this energy because of nature and its durability to withstand massive manipulation.

For this to work, the soul needs to disconnect from spirit. Saturn and Mars have experienced these manipulations or so they would be perfect to guide earth through the negative zone.

To give you further details on how this manipulation works, the souls that are connected to the higher dimensions, when they incarnate on earth, feel the effects of the negative architecture more than anyone else.

Now if you ease into the third dimension from fourth, the effects are hard but not as hard. If you see or feel negative creatures of lower astral, you came from the higher dimensions into earth.

The old world of Saturn is a society that is free but also hard on itself. Like the Roman empire without the murderous conflict from a dictator. That does not mean it was not tough on its citizens to be perfect, to do the best they can.

With a big brother society keeping an eye on everyone, it was mostly about your progress and what you could bring to society to improve it. Arnold Schwarzenegger is from Saturn to give you a better idea. Notice how prolific he is in his own life.

Building the perfect life and body, he would be seen as a great leader on Saturn. He never applied himself to be a leader on Saturn, but the lessons stayed with him. On earth he saw nothing but opportunity. He applied the Saturn technic, and even to this day he still does. This goes for his timeline, which he altered all the time, and that was intentional before he incarnated.

Aliens and the Ascension

A new version of earth is upon us. Timelines are moving to the higher dimensions. Getting to know your universe is what you are going to experience next. The fifth dimension is around the corner. How to connect with the fifth dimension is simple. Remember, life is a dream.

In a dream, you can do anything. Bring that into the third dimension. Over time you will see the mechanics of third dimension more clearly. And you will even see your illuminati. They know what you know. They are watching you but not what you think.

The reptilians are here to bring you down, to keep you in the matrix mindset. As you clear the negative manipulations, life will become more clear. You will begin to see the edges of the timeline vortex as a new timeline comes into your life. You already feel the vibrations of this experience when change is in the air.

New changes will become more clear when the time is right. As your energies leave the third dimension, you will see more.

As you enter the fifth dimension, the understanding of law of attraction will become more clear. It will come faster, and knowledge will find you easily. Moving through the dimensions will be as easy as a single thought.

Some might get jealous as you come and go as you please and others cannot. The lower third dimension will have humans that will never want to evolve. Success is found in the third dimension. Most won't want to leave. They will find every excuse to hold on.

The century of magic will begin.

Souls that wish to ascend to the fifth dimension will continue to learn of their higher abilities, and even train others in the fourth to connect to the fifth.

Are you selfless? Do you care about others? With no money as a motivation, you will ascend faster than those who have motivations of wealth.

Moving through the dimensions will come easy as you get used to it. The year 2019 is the year of the awakening. 2020 is the year of Atlantis. Humanity will see further into themselves and see the complex vortexes around the earth. Realize lower energies can no longer both you are they used too.

Even the illuminati will see you as an exceptional soul. And of course, there will be exceptions, where lessons are one after the other with no end to the lessons. Some of these humans have karma before they can ascend.

You must understand as a galactic human, the third dimension will not understand you. The archon manipulation has them on their platter. So the third dimension is on a wheel of ascension you no longer belong to. Some will be of the fourth dimension and be controlled by ego and telling you that ego is controlling you, when in truth it's controlling them.

The fifth dimension will glow, will feel like home. Realize you will be protected. Once again lower vibrations can't communicate in the fifth. So they won't see you.

You will see reptilians and zetas, for example, moving through the third. Earth will never look the same. It will feel like the third dimension is as simple as turning a page.

Being in the fifth dimension, you will just know what to do. There will be a slight learning curve such as keeping your vibration high.

Let's put it this way. When you feel the third dimension no longer has purpose, you will continue to close it down within yourself. You might feel less emotional. Everyone is different in this experience. You will feel love. You will feel unconditional love beyond third-dimension experiences.

As for alien disclosure contact, you will be with the aliens during this. There's a possibility you will feel or see other versions of yourself in different dimensions.

Illuminati Church in Astral

As humanity upgrades, it energizes the illuminati and will no longer exist on your planet. The control grid around the planet is healing. The illuminati have not truly left the planet. Their influence and mind control still exists until humanity releases it.

The elite want to watch and see what happens. They want to grow with humanity after thousands of years of bloodshed.

There are two kinds of happiness: a third-dimensional happiness, which usually has materialism accompany it. Then there is fourth-dimension happiness where the physical world no longer exists.

Connecting to the higher energies will give you more insight into the universe.

The watershed of experience is when humanity connects to the higher energies. High vibrations are finally recognized and utilized to use your spirit in a positive way, where you can easily change your reality and move through the dimensions.

Humanity will have difficulty hearing this now. Because of the illuminati, prison is around you. The illuminati sanctuary is where you are now. Some of you might feel like you have been released from it. See the people in the seats watching the illuminati ritual. This ritual continues the third-dimension traditions.

You can be released from your illuminati contract. The more loving you are, the better. The more judgmental and angry you become, the harder it is to be released. Everyone, almost everyone, is in the illuminati illusion of third dimension. The matrix program was created by them and can be easily released if you are kind.

Yes, they are connected to atrocities of the planet. They are also connected to the positivity connected to the planet also.

This is what the illuminati sanctuary looks like. Think of a Catholic Church with illuminati symbolism instead of religious symbols. Gold is everywhere and just beautiful. Humanity is in this sanctuary. Billions of people are in this sanctuary every day and all day.

The illuminati do rituals in front of the congregation. To give you a perspective, this ritual goes on all day long. You can come and go, but all souls are connected to this dimension. There are several names of this dimension. The zero dimension is easy enough to understand and remember. The illuminati dimension is another name you can use.

Realize the symbolism is much different in this world. Also humanity gives the illuminati power to conduct this power. If you ask for torture, they will give you torture. If you ask for rape, they will give you rape, and this has been going on for thousands of years.

They go through this pain with you. Some of your parents are with the illuminati consciousness to bring this darkness to your world.

Darkness is here to strengthen the weak. The muscle of humanity is here to strengthen and take back the earth they easily gave away. The Atlanteans were very powerful but weak in so many ways. To strengthen was to give away their power, to shut down the fourth-dimensional earth.

The third-dimension mindset is in the illuminati church, the rules of earth and conditions. A hidden royalty is there but never seen easily. This is the real world. The fourth dimension is where you are working to unlock yourself from the third.

You wonder what is beyond the third dimension? Another version of you is there waiting for you to integrate into the fourth, a world within a world because of so many dimensions. Not everyone is meant to see this right away because the curse of the third dimension is still needed for soul growth.

As you integrate into the fourth, you will just know what is going on. The knowledge will just come to you. The third dimension will be like a ghost world, and to some this is already happening.

Connecting with spirit is to just let it flow.

As you adjust you will see more.

Illuminati Castle in Astral

The Illuminati Castle explained. This is where you come for an upgrade of the soul. The illuminati castle is where the true test of the soul is experienced. Some do integrate into the illuminati and become a super soldier. Once again, this is one of the places the soul can visit and incarnate through to bring heavy enhancements to oneself.

Those in the third dimension won't believe it at first. This is higher learning of the soul in the fourth dimension and even the fifth, to see the world as it truly is simple to find. Connect to the fourth dimension and you will see it all.

The kings of Atlantis are in the fourth dimension. Humanity wants research but realizes a great amount of knowledge has been destroyed. As you integrate into the fourth dimension, knowledge will become easy to access.

Not just the akashic records but more.

When the world needs your fourth dimensional energy, you will go through an upgrade. To go further you are each other. Your consciousness interconnects. You are each other, a world family that has trouble getting along. That will one day change.

The wars on the battlefield and in the family are connected to the illuminati castle. You might see the illuminati as bird people or not even human. Let the knowledge flow as you slowly upgrade to the higher dimensions.

To be a king of England or queen, you must go through the illuminati castle and be heavily tested, such as reincarnate on worlds you disagree with, before the earth incarnation, because earth is the final prize.

Being chosen for earth in a high-profile position such as king or queen is not taken lightly. Why do you think Queen Elizabeth is still holding onto the position? The reptilian overlords work through her, and this is most likely her last chance as queen anywhere in the universe.

At this moment she has dozens of queen positions on other worlds. There are fifteen lifetimes connecting this world at the moment.

Do you believe someone like this would ever be allowed to be in a royalty position again? Elizabeth is queen of the prison planet, controlled by a secret society and unwilling to give up her position.

Fear of the unknown–your Vladimir Putin is slightly afraid of the queen and what she is hiding. Afraid might not be the best word so uncomfortable is probably a better word. The reptilians around Putin are nowhere as aggressive as Queen Elizabeth.

The alien public relations department is doing their best with the queen, to make her as likeable as possible, even through behind closed doors she is a completely different person.

As the human consciousness increases, you will see parallel worlds, such as London being connected to another planet, the pyramids of Egypt on a Syrian world. Humanity in the future will activate the pyramids. There will be star children that will know how to do it. The alien energies of your planet will increase.

There will be a generation of people that will incarnate on earth and have a fourth- and fifth-dimension energy. They will know all and be all. They will be here to reactivate the planet.

There will be a divide also as humanity realizes its galactic origins. Humanity will go through a culture shock that it won't be able to handle. As the fourth dimension increases its energies, the fall of the third dimension will begin to truly show its demise.

Kings will no longer be kings. The media will eventually fall. It will be a shadow of itself. Your future ancestors will go through hell and enlightenment like no other, removing the human element and connecting more with the alien DNA within. The future generations will be like no other. History will be erased because of the corruption, no longer needed as the energies increase worldwide.

When the pyramids are reactive, it's over for the dark illuminati.

Are there battles in the illuminati castle? Yes, indeed there are, but they are energy conflicts. This is where souls can also go from light to dark, just in the castle alone.

They change their timeline on earth to be more money-obsessed or power-obsessed–can cause drug addiction and other vices for the soul on earth to lose control. Temptations on earth cause the disruption in the timeline.

The soul in astral fights to stay positive, but as the human on earth connected to that soul falls to the dark side, the astral soul falls into a grey area, an area of manipulation that can cause more disruption.

Realize your astral self stays strong. Even with the interference, they adjust to the earth human decisions. The lessons of earth are significant before you return to spirit. In life, change going into darkness will usually span for seven to eight lifetimes on earth if you wish to return.

For example, you turn to a life of murder and cannot release that contract. You will reincarnate with a darker energy. Many reptilians and other low-vibration beings expand on that darkness in different experiences.

Some souls incarnate as archons and contribute through their vibration. What is funny about the archon is that the soul can release the negativity easier than a human incarnation. Archon has an entirely different point of view than any other alien being.

Notice the negative television shows and examples of negativity. That is there to show you that you are not alone, which makes it harder to release the temptations of darkness.

As an alien being such as Pleiadian and Arcturian, you take advantage of other beings, show their weaknesses, continue with darkness until it no longer serves you.

The archons turn others into darkness. They do have their dark lords of mind manipulation, manipulating all beings and pulling them into their collective. What is it that scares you? The archons will connect to it.

They don't see darkness the way humans do. They see it as an experience, unemotional scientists that want to see what will make you or break you.

They can replicate an Arcturian world and all seems fine until you notice the inconsistencies. The world is just a projection and a trap.

Want an example? Just look at your dimension.

Alien Disclosure

The planets in your solar system, Saturn, Uranus, and even Pluto, have beings on earth assisting in the ascension. The beings of Pluto weren't always helpful. When their world was destroyed, they blamed earth.

The perfect utopia was ruined by their own creations. Experimenting and not paying attention to the details led to the destruction of their planet.

Beings of Pluto can be very powerful psychically. They even give you physical pain by using their minds. The reason we are bringing this up is because disclosure is right around the corner. The time frame might not be as quickly as some would like, such as right now. In other timelines it is happening. One world after the other is going through disclosure. And those worlds connecting planet earth isn't too far down the line of the queue.

Knowledge is power, and this knowledge will bring you closer to the fourth dimension. The earth's consciousness is around third dimension or lower, depending on the mind control the human will allow in their energy field.

It is true that only a few are needed to allow disclosure to occur on your planet–making that link to the higher dimensions.

The fifth dimension's energies will synchronize with the alien vibrations. New energies will be brought to the earth–building layers of new energies, and that will consume the earth. Basically the connections with aliens and humans will improve.

The layer between the third and fourth dimensions will thin. When humans let go of the possibility they are alone, the vibrations will increase. The strength between humans and aliens is increasing for contact.

The timeline for when this will happen is constantly in flux. As you think about it and want it, the vibration strengthens. You are now receiving the information on how to handle the contact. Sightings in the skies will increase as more humans want it but also understand who they are connecting to.

The thought of alien contact is unheard of in your generation. It's time to change that way of thinking. The energy for contact is to happen now. Allow the energy to connect with you. Enhance your abilities to connect with your guides. Open the dream world of your imagination.

Your dream world is your astral and alien world.

Contact with aliens is already happening. Everyone has contact with the alien world. Bringing this vibration into the physical and nonphysical is where you are heading.

Timeline connections with aliens are getting closer.

The conflict comes in who is making contact. Who are these aliens? Are they Pleiadian, Sirian, Zeta Grey, Yahyel, or Reptilian? The answer is all of these and more. First contact will bring a change in energies and awareness. The following contact will change the earth completely.

September 2018 is just the beginning of a new phase on earth. Alien awareness will increase through the years. More information will come through to help make clear who you are connecting to. To be clear, many of you will connect to all of the beings.

What will come next is to see yourself as an alien being–basically seeing your alien origins. Many of you are connected to aliens no one has ever heard of.

Look at a mirror, and in the reflection you see a Blue Avian or a gorilla being. Upgrading to the fifth dimension will come gradually. As the third dimension shifts out of existence, more knowledge of your Atlantean roots will emerge.

The tidal wave of awareness will emerge.

Basically many of you will shift into higher consciousness. Realize no drama in this consciousness, only unconditional love. It will have its conflict but not the third-dimensional kind of mindset.

The humans in third dimension are putting their heads in the sand as they know what is coming. So causing conflict is all they understand, the rapture of the third dimension. As your society slowly upgrades, those used to the old ways of life are not going to like the new changes.

The power within will begin to unite, a spiritual upgrade where you feel your chakras for the first time. They will come more to life than ever before. Feel them turn, and as your thoughts move through your mind, you will feel the chakra energy through your body and even feel the chakras move.

If you already feel you are on two worlds, that feeling will increase.

Sounds and objects around you will feel very different as the mass will shift around you. Ever have a chair speak to you? Ever have a conversation with the sky?

Many of you will have different experiences. It's all part of your own personal awakening.

The Martian and Saturn agendas will come more clear. The illuminati will be more understood. Fear of the unknown will vibrate into another dimension. You will be free of fear if you can handle the experience–stepping out of one world into another.

Want disclosure? Heal the pain of the old world. Heal the divide between humans, even though understanding of the alien presence is divided because of the belief system. Not to say everyone has to agree; there will always be a difference of opinion.

Healing the third-dimensional timeline–the violence that is sparked by Archon agendas. The test of time is to move above the manipulations.

The cooling of violence on your planet will show the higher dimensions are coming through, connecting to the weather anomalies and healing the forces of nature, such as lowering the strength of a hurricane, extending the daylight for a few more hours, connecting with mother earth to assist with the daily rainfall. Some people will make it their life to connect with nature, not just in their area but around the world–feeling the energies of Switzerland or the Netherlands.

Your job will be attending to the earth, connecting with the earth, feeling peace with yourself, raising the earth's vibration through nature, changing the colors of the trees and grass of nature, purifying the planet with high vibrations as humanity moves to the new earth.

How does this begin? Recognize the alien within.

Alien Species Introduction

As humanity goes through a vibrational upgrade, many changes will be made, such as understanding the alien species on your planet, the strangeness of it all and the realization that this is a channeled message – a channeled message connecting to the universe to open the heavens of your earth to a new way of life. Understand that much of your bible has been channeled.

Uplifting messages and changes to your vibration are needed. New information to your planet is needed as you enhance your way of life.

In this segment, we will be connecting to Alpha Centauri. This star system is assisting earth, but not much is known of its assistance.

Realize that major events on your planet also cause alien reentry into your world. With each event, human consciousness allows it to happen. There are major events happening across earth all the time, throughout the ages. That's a lot of alien beings connected to your reality.

Even with the contract with third dimension, thousands of years of integrations have been made. You wake up with the earth everyday and never realize the complications it takes to put the third dimensional reality together.

Several matrix energies are seeded on your world, so they are added or replaced when needed. As a new era arrives, changes are made to the matrix. Every second a change is made. Your future is planned before you incarnate. Think of it as a highway system – a complex map of highways and you are the car. The vehicle with the free will to do whatever you want. But there are times when you can't just get off a life path. When life gets difficult, it's hard to end the difficulties, correct? It feels like the difficulties are never ending.

When you are living a harsh reality, the timeline feels like forever. This is the most crucial time, because the soul expands with never ending information. The soul can even turn to a golden color if you ever thought to look.

A golden energy at the right level gives the soul connections to the spirit world. During this battle with the third dimension, higher dimensional beings are here to connect. The harsh reality opens you up to higher beings because you need all the help you can get.

The easier the life, the more likely the soul will play it safe and not grow.

The harsher the reality, the more risks are made because there is no other choice. Which gives your life a complexity. During the turmoil, it's not always easy to connect. During the rough weather of soul expansion, it's not always easy to see through the weather and to connect to the sunshine of high vibrational energies.

Every human has about a thousand alien species connected to them for one single incarnation. In the third dimension, it's hard to imagine this. In higher dimensions, it makes so much sense. Think of yourself as a cruise ship heading out to sea. You need all the help you can get.

Your higher self is the captain and your shipmates are your guides. For some of you, your main guide is your higher self. For those who never have an issue with their guides, most likely your higher self is your guide.

The main spirit guide is like a executive chef at a restaurant, making sure everything runs smoothly. Hard tests are there to make sure you make it through.

So with so many guides, most are alien beings. Close your eyes and what do you see? The belief system can make it hard to see the guides. Humans feel they are not worthy. Everyone is worthy.

Not everyone is ready to see a spirit guide. Some of the most powerful guides are insectoids. When you go into the darkness of your timeline, the insectoid guide is there with you.

To give you a perspective of the Alpha Centauri aliens, they are on earth to make sure humanity doesn't destroy other planets. The illuminati consciousness wants to rid of aliens assisting humanity. Galactic wars are common in channelings.

The news media is manipulated because the aliens are losing control over the human mind. They hit the fear factor and control the narrative. Those in the third dimension don't notice it; business as usual, they think. These are the same humans that think you are alone in the universe.

Think again.

The Rhinoceros From Sirius

Realize that the rhino live in many star systems. Sirius is connected to earth, which brought their energy to your world. This is a war alien species but also a peaceful vibration. They have fought the canines for millions of years for who can be the dominant species.

The rhino has defeated the reptilian countless times.

The rhino has found peace among their species, but it wasn't easy. They are descendants of the dragon race. They no longer carry reptilian DNA. The dragon is part of their soul evolution. Shifting dimensions and awakening forgotten worlds. Assisting them with finding new life to reincarnate.

They, like you, always felt they were the only life in the universe. All alien species have a evolution of being alone as they advance in maturity. Wars with the monkeys and destruction of many reptilian planets.

Millions of years of wars through this universe. The destruction of planets is felt on your world because earth houses many of the refugees. Have a problem with the reptilians? Call in the rhinos.

The elephant and rhino share their DNA, as you can see the similarities. For a long time, the rhinos protected the elephants from the reptilians and insectoids. As the elephant race became a peaceful race, they no longer accepted war.

Many alien species saw this as a weakness, and used the volunerbility to their advantage.

The rhino arrived on your planet to learn and expand their own consciousness. Most of them evolved from emotion. The passions also evolved, and as they evolved back into passion, they once again began to dominate other species.

The rhino is similar to the reptilians, showing strength and dominating other races.

Much of this thinking is now in the past. But as the rhino connected to the earth human experience, their civilization changed. Every species is here to evolve to better themselves. Making peace with the insectoids. Surviving the mind control of the insectoids.

Rhino worlds for millions of years were under the control of the insectoids and the rabbit species. Warrior races sometimes believe they carry all the knowledge similar to your planet. When the truth of manipulation is revealed, those souls are either ridiculed or destroyed.

The rhino is still evolving into a peaceful vibration. They are the protectors of the universe. They incarnated on earth to evolve and now the reptilian manipulation has removed them from your planet. The survival skills of the rhino was inherited by the human race, as they are one of many alien races watching over your planet, protecting it.

When connecting to your alien friends, you might see a humanoid rhino being on ship. Their peaceful energy is giving guidance. Many have left the energies of war. With their knowledge, they can cure negativity and remove insectoid implants.

Simplicity is of their species. Notice the complications of your world. The more simplistic and less negative it becomes. The more enlightened it will be with simplicity.

They have similar worlds that are the same as your third dimension. It's more primitive, but they have vehicles and barter practices.

One of the reasons they came to earth was to protect humanity from the reptilian and archon manipulations. A human species that doesn't know any better needs someone to watch out for them.

Usually, rhinos appear at government alien meetings with humans. They normally don't say anything but their presence is known sometimes. The illuminati puts pressure on humanity to grow. The rhino is here to give some relief.

Rhinos are here to shift humanity out of war and into peace. We are here to assist with your ascension and be recognized as your family.

At this time, the rhinos are watching over the earth's oceans. Portals are used within the oceans to manipulate humanity, and unwanted guests arrived through the Atlantic and the Pacific religions.

Antarctica is protected at this time.

The Gnomes

The gnomes are the creators of Agartha. Magician gnomes come from the twelfth dimension. Yes, there are higher dimensions. Basically, Agartha, also called your middle earth, comes from another star system, which is in Sirius.

The birthplace of your planet came from Agartha. The formation of your world and its habitat is from Agartha. Earth is connected to several universes, as is every living creature on your planet. Agartha took earth under its arm as the planet was being created.

The gnomes are from another star system in another universe so opposite from your own. They have seen the highest of light and the darkest of dark. On other worlds they are tall, and on your planet, most are short.

They assisted in the creation of the human race. The human had been created long before the the Lyrans connected to its energies. But for the Lyrans to channel the human vibrations into your universe was a fascinating experience.

Every alien species has help in their evolution. Have you ever thought about how a twelfth dimensional being can become a physical third dimensional being? With trillions of years of evolution and a soul desire for exploration?

The break away into the third dimension was not easy. The gnomes were one of the first beings to do so. At the time, they did not have a physical form. Reincarnation downgrades one's experience into the lower dimensions.

Without reincarnation this could never happen.

Reincarnation can be called breakaway. Dimensions are created to protect the third dimension in case of fall out. Your reality can easily break down and cause a mental depression. Depression is caused by dimensions being tampered with.

Weather conflicts can also be caused by disruptions in the dimensions.

Realize gnomes weren't always human. They adapted this experience as earth became habitable. In other dimensions and universes, they were humanoid Gnomes. Many of them appeared as statues. Ever heard of movable statues?

68

Many of the early wizards were gnomes. The ancient gnomes are connected to the Nordic Tall Blonde Aliens. Many gnomes incarnated as the first ancient Atlanteans.

The gnome magic can be connected, too. Humanity is a lost species because of manipulation. A call for higher dimensions will clear the blockages of your earth. Acknowledge the power within. Everyone is a magician. Many aren't ready for the responsibility.

Think of a society of magicians. The gnome vibration lives within the trees and all of nature. Ask them to come out. Ask them to say hello. They are playful and carry an organic wisdom that will live with you for centuries.

Those that know spirituality usually carry a gnome vibration with them.

The Gorilla's From Another Universe

The gorilla, or ape, comes from another universe. As the species evolved, other alien life adapted to their body structure. This wasn't always recognized as a positive connection. Worlds, and even universes, were destroyed because of the misuse of their genetics.

Gorillas are a highly evolved alien species that usually keep to themselves. They battled the Carian eagle races for millions of years. Causing earthquakes and other technologies to rupture a planet were created by gorillas. Go for the planet's core.

Removing a planet from a solar system was never hard. As this species evolved, they connected to all solar systems – at least the majority of them in your universe. There are areas where they are no longer welcomed.

With the creation of a savage reptilian, the gorillas came very close to pulling the reptilians into extinction timelines. The war between gorillas and reptilians continues on. Humanity evolves with the ape reptilian on earth. To have a human with a reptilian brain was unheard of.

Ancient battles with the felines created a relationship with gorillas, using their DNA for human genetic projects. With the gorillas realizing they can't defeat the felines, a close relationship was created.

The felines adapted early to gorilla DNA as they became more humanoid. In the beginning, the gorillas saw this as illegal. With each war, gorilla DNA spread across the universe. The Carians used this as an opportunity to change their appearance into a humanoid experience.

Not all aliens get along, and that's the point of evolution. The creation of earth was built with imperfections. The ape is a protector of earth. We seed plants and we destroy them. Earth is needed for the advancement of many alien species. Like it or not, they are learning from humanity.

For as long as it takes, the more you know and understand the further aware your earth becomes of the alien species crowding your planet. The champions are earth humans, and they are here to take the universe into a new phase of life.

Similar to humans, apes don't always get along with each other. An ape connected to artificial intelligence can cause havoc, and it has. Yes, we have been involved with the greys. Where do you think their form comes from? There are always going to be different perspectives.

This is your graduation present as you evolve from the third dimension.

The ape has ruled over feline worlds. The apes have inhabited two worlds and destroyed them both because of their differences of opinion. The apes are far superior to the martians for military tactics. The more spiritual apes are normally of different colors: purples, greens and yellow, to name a few.

They are normally born of a certain color to reflect their vibration. The arcturians assisted in the apes' evolution into spiritual understanding.

Humanity as you know it is still just a youngster. But we as aliens can learn so much from you. Yes, you are still a young race of people on earth. But there is so much you have not discovered about yourselves. As the soul awakens into a pure understanding, the knowledge of the universe will come easily.

The apes, the canine and the feline have evolved enough to assist in your upbringing. You can say we have seen it all. Your world has brought more challenges. Like a parent breaking down in panic, sometimes we don't know what to do, so we seek help. This is why the carians and other alien species have inhabited your planet.

Aliens don't have all the answers.

The reason why our worlds were destroyed was because of separation. We didn't agree, and so war broke out and never ended. And resources were ruined. Strangely enough, you have the same individuals in your government that started the wars in our world.

What broke us apart was how we lived. As our resources were being strained, we tried to use quick tactics to fix a problem. Look at your current power grid, for example. Some wanted to renew the energies by building new facilities; others said no. Simple repairs that would be quicker was the solution, but that decision cost us lives.

Over time, war broke out and once the war began, there was no end.

We normally keep our world's primitive living in nature. Crystal materials as energy sources to light the skies with high vibration. Realize, at the higher dimensions, that conflict doesn't exist as it does on your world.

We collect information, such as insectoid clothing and technologies they are willing to share from other worlds, and bring it to our culture.. An exchange helps us all evolve. As we develop new species, you can say it's similar to releasing a new car.

There's more sophistication and love that goes into it. As we slow down in our own evolution, we create. We learn from new alien beings. Taking a frog and feline and splicing them together creates a new species.

With this new species, we grow and ascend into the higher dimensions. Some of the creations carry on our karma, for better or for worse. Alien species come and go.

The ape will live forever.

A DNA split can cause havoc on an alien species. With so many different species, connecting to one single species can cause tremors in the universe. With too many DNA stains from different aliens, the mental functionality can be fatal.

Reptilians go through this all the time; too many aliens in one species of alien, basically. A reptilian with too much arcturian and feline can become mentally entangled. Reptilians and apes have come close to the annunaki creation process.

It's just never the same, but both species have come close. You can say the annunaki DNA recipe is finer than that of the apes and reptilians. Similar to a famous chef, every chef has his/her own speciality that no one can match.

It's all a point of view in the long run. Apes are known for creating spices with fur and humanoid figure. And reptilians are known for snake-like skin and a rough exterior. The orangutan is a popular leader among the ape communities. They are normally never ignored and seen as almost a deity of knowledge.

Orangutans aren't known for war. They are known for a simple and economic good life. Barter is the most with the alien races. That term isn't used, but you have an idea; basically, the exchange for service and goods. Aliens help each other and, most of the time, it goes very well. But not always, as you have seen on your world with money exchange.

To give you another perspective, one reason why money is seen as bad in the spiritual community is party because many alien beings that are incarnated on earth want nothing to do with money. So, taking money is seen as evil or villianous.

Money is just another exchange of energy. And yes, it has occult energies around it but it is necessary for survival at the moment.

Spiritual development has never been easy on earth. In many ways, it's a lose/lose situation.

Being a fourth dimensional alien is easier than being a third dimensional human. Rising out of the ashes of manipulation is never easy. Humanity on earth has taken on the karmic debt of other alien species, such as pigs.

Ape have been abducted and had their DNA altered where they are only skin and no hair. A hairless ape, basically, and the pigs do this to mark their territory. The battle between apes and pigs has gone on since the inception of this universe.

In some ways, you say humans are teaching pigs a lesson by eating pigs. Look at your dinner plate and notice ape for dinner is very rare. But as for the pig, that is another story.

The current apes incarnated as humans on your world are usually in wrestling. Rock climbers have a lot of ape DNA. Scientists that enjoy the jungles have a great amount of ape connections. To give you another perspective, those chefs famous or not are also known for DNA splicing.

Aliens in the higher densities normally don't cook other species. But those that are used to combine DNA choose cooking or knitting as another form of creation.

Understand a world can have information overload. Too much information can quickly slow a world down during the ascension of understanding oneself. Apes can be seen on your world, and yes – they do wear primitive clothing, like an old fashion western, they prefer the simple ways of life.

Yes, in the old west, was not easy, but it is an ape's world you are looking at. Not to say they will be walking around in a cowboy hat. That depends on the ape being. Apes are known to carry weapons, but on your world, they most likely won't appear carrying a weapon.

Think of an old-fashioned space western and you will connect to the apes.

The Pigs

One of the originating places of the pigs is Alpha Centauri. Basically they come from many different places. The pigs have blocked energies from earth. They have seeded planets that later destroyed themselves. Basically because of a lack of love.

The pigs create and move on. Many alien species cannot understand the pigs for the life of them. They don't even know what they want most of the time. Wonder why pigs on you're planet eat so much? They want energy and they want it all. In your world, the pig animal is far from perfect, but in the long run, it is pretty hilarious.

Humans on earth get much of their sense of humor from the pigs. A sense of humor that makes zero sense is pig humor. They don't want to be understood and most want to party. Have kids and party with the kids. They are world explorers and creating civilizations is kind of boring to some of them.

You can say the pigs were kind of forced to help humanity. They really wanted nothing to do with humans. The felines added the pigskin DNA to the modern earth human. The pigs didn't have a problem with that but the reptilians did. Many galactic wars just with that simple add on for the human race.

The pig alien species have their own human-like civilizations. Most of these worlds are primitive but very advanced in technology. There are billions of different kinds of pig species.

The warthog is known as the warrior race. Similar to humans, they can be conquerors. Pigs are known for creating moons and destroying them. Some are very similar to humans in regards to sexual breeding positions.

The pigs try everything and aren't afraid of failure. They are also known for being very advantageous – they climb mountains and deep sea dive. Look at the modern earth human and visualize a pig nose.

This kind of pig human has been around for billions of years. Understand also that the pigs were working on human genetics. The pig and the ape have worked together creating different species of human since before the felines created the earth human.

The feline created the human, populated Sirius and the Pleiades, and so on.

The story of the felines originating the human isn't really true. The human created by the felines was popular and became the mainframe work for a human species. But the felines were not the first.

There are ape-like beings with pig heads. Some are causing issues in the universe and aren't allowed around the earth. Are pigs causing difficulties on earth?

You know the turn party animal? That term comes from the pigs. Indulgence of drinking and partying is the pig way. Self-destructive pigs do exist. Some fat CEOs on your planet are pigs.

Party pigs take over worlds so they can party. They can get kicked off of worlds and so they look for another hangout. Some can be fun and others can be destructive.

There are worlds and dimensions where the pigs are similar to the greys – very violent and mechanical in their ways. Shutting down ships and taking over planets to increase their population. Adding their DNA to as many species as they can to show their dominance and to secure the existence of their species.

There are military pigs in the universe, where there are only animal aliens and no humans. The knowledge of a human, or even seeing one, is very rare. On some worlds where a human is captured from a world such as yours, the humans are put on display. There are several sides of the pigs. Some are very friendly and others are war-like.

At one time, they once dominated the human race on your planet. You can say your skin is a layer of manipulation and the body is a cage. As you activate the higher dimensions within yourself, you will see your skin alter to a more thin and vibrant energy where you can even connect to your own skin and feel the organs inside of your body.

Instead of blood, you will feel a light force. Energy field and it will be a high. You will feel like you are on drugs and it will be the best feeling you have ever felt.

The Military And The Matrix

The military we see cross our world is not to keep us safe from foreign invaders. The military is here to continue the matrix of our reality. The aerospace companies, such as Boeing and Lockheed Martin, received a lot more money from the government than what is publicly disclosed.

These military contract companies control the government and operate in secret of their true intentions. Contract companies are created all the time to deceive the public. If one single company received all the contracts that would be an easy red flag. So, the companies are created, but in the long run, are controlled in secret by the ruling elite.

The military keeps humanity in a matrix setting. They say the military is here to keep humanity safe, when in truth they are enslaving humanity. Many of these military contractors are in control of the world. The majority of the chakras of humanity have been altered and damaged by the radiation used on the planet – microwave technologies, from cell phones to radar. Finding proof in the physical world is the problem if you don't have military clearance.

There is a shadow side of the military that knows everything about everyone and they are helped by the dark elite. Negative reptilians is one group, but there are many.

Many of the news reporters you see on the major networks do not even have souls; instead they have mental implants to keep them going. Even famous radio personalities have been manipulated to continue the matrix agenda. Psychic agenda is upon us. Connecting to your guides and higher spirits will assist with the earth clearing out the matrix manipulations. As the awakening continues, the control grid will loosen.

There are military bases all across the world and they are for the higher elites to keep humanity captive. Hollywood and others means of entertainment are used to continue the seduction. The positive elite are assisting with the awakening and patience is needed.

The military has ruled humanity ever since Roman times. The Vatican has a military presence that requires militaries around the world to follow certain guidelines. Major corporations, like Disney, are spending a great deal of money on their theme parks to continue the matrix manipulation.

They say it's to make money but in truth, it's to keep the fantasy of the third dimension reality in its continued flux. The comforts of the third dimension will slowly begin to dissolve. Most people will be in denial, but as the truth increases, a third dimensional shake down will occur. Many life changes will happen for the better.

Many who don't want change and want the life of materialism will have difficulties releasing the programing.

These large companies also get penalized for not keeping people in the matrix. Their stock goes down and huge layoffs follow. They must continue to motivate and keep the human population seduced by new products and matrix propaganda.

What are the true humans? The true humans are free to go and do whatever they want to invent and share their talent, and most importantly, to live a good life.

In this current world, each birth creates an instant slave. The manipulations begin on day one with attacks from the darker forces. If you are going to be on this planet, you will go by their rules.

This mindset will change.

Parents will learn from the children, with the family growing together and building on their talents and creating a better world for everyone.

A new frame of mind will enter the human consciousness.

The Pentagon in Washington is the center of all of this. As there are many shadow government bases underground, the Pentagon is the stage where many of the missions are deployed. The wealthy elite use the Pentagon for war games across the planet.

Just visualize a wealthy elitist with nothing to do on a Saturday night. He calls the Pentagon to deploy troops somewhere only because the elitist wants to impress a girlfriend or use the military for revenge against a known enemy.

The creation of ISIS and other forms of manufactured terrorism is all an elitis game.

The military industrial complex is used against humanity. It's not here to serve humanity in any way. It serves only the wealthy to gain more power and shut down human consciousness. Connecting to your guides and higher consciousness will give you an understanding of the whole picture.

They use weapons against humanity to cause violence and fires. Once humanity realizes the truth, the awakening will increase across the planet. The removal of the military will increase the energies of the ascension and bring in the new earth.

Until then, psychic wars will increase and answers to questions will finally be revealed. Intuitives will be able to tap into the consciousness of the Illuminati and be able to understand it. To shut down the dark forces, one needs to understand how they work. And understand how to release their manipulations.

The majority of humans are treated like caged animals. The fifth dimension can only be achieved by letting go of the old teachings. The elite are the main cause of the world's problems. Unfortunately, humanity has lost itself to continue the manipulations – by bowing down to its religions and falling for greed mailupulations.

The military continues the matrix energies. The souls trapped in the incarnation cycles are in the billions. This current life is a continuation of the last incarnation. Not all souls trapped in this cycle are from earth. They transitioned from other slave worlds similar to this planet.

As earth goes into an upgrade process, the chance of release is very possible from the paradox incarnation cycle. Religious cults and other aspects of spiritual confinement will continue the paradox cycle of incarnations. There are ways out of the cycles by breaking away from these cults of manipulation.

Buddhism is an example. Buddhism isn't perfect, but it allows the soul to release from old contracts and find peace. It also allows on to be curious without falling for restrictions from others; being yourself and being free and making your own rules. Believe in what is best for you. Connect to the reality that brings comfort into your life.

The elite use humanity for slavery but this won't last forever. They also keep the infrastructure of life together until humanity takes back the planet. Until the human race reconnects to its full power, the current environment will continue.

Remove the hate and paranoia and what do you have? Hopefully you will find love for yourself and have gratitude towards others. Connect to your guides and higher spirit angels. Advance through the timelines and evolve to your fullest potential.

Find peace within yourself and let your curiosity go beyond this dimension. Connect to the universe and allow your higher self energies to flow through you more evenly. Advance in intuitive energies and find a fluid balance.

Disconnect from the third dimension manipulations and connect to higher spirit energies.

Unlock the matrix. Unlock the fear. Reinvent the human.

Go beyond the physical realities and connect to the higher astral beings. Higher astral beings are there for your wellness. Open your crown chakra and connect to the higher realms beyond this earth's lower astral dimensions.

The knowledge of the lower astral is needed, but that doesn't mean you can't rise above it. Some can't rise above and that is called modern reality.

Higher astral energies will heal the third dimension through your actions and thoughts. Higher source energy will help your abilities grow. Feel your intuitive energies heal. Wisdom comes in different forms. You don't need to see the future. All timelines are happening now. How you feel now will affect the future. So, technically you can see the future if you know how to look for it.

The future and past are now. Everything is now. Removing time can be done.

Rise above this dimension. Rise to the astral plane. Look at the earth from astral.

What do you see?

Do you see reptilians around the military bases? Do you see Zeta Greys around technology? Many Sirian's incarnate as a Zeta and carry on the knowledge through a human incarnation. Some humans seem very robotic when inventing technology.

Modern technology is channeled by humans. Why is humanity so connected to phones? On other worlds, connecting to technology is very normal. As you connect with your phone, you become more alien. Yes – the phone can take you over. When you chat with someone on the other line, either on phone or computer, you are connecting to their energy.

As humanity opens up, you will realize you are inside that person's mind, hearing the thoughts they want you to hear. Opening the telepathic portal is essential for soul advancement, and it's happening now.

Interdimensional Shape Beings

Ever think about a reality where shapes were the dominant species?

Ever have a conversation with a box? Where do these shapes come from? They come from another universe where objects are king. Shapes of all kinds are constantly creating forms. A fluid reality where a box is king.

Where a box becomes a dominant species over other shapes.

Welcome to the fifth dimension.

This is an introduction to the box people. Think of a human with a box for a head. There are no features such as eyes or ears. Sure, you can place a hat on his or her head. The human body consumed the box world.

What is it? What to do with a human form?

You can call them the box people. Call them whatever you want. They have been watching your world for a very long time. Think of societies of humans with box heads, circle heads, triangle heads and so on.

Notice the skyscrapers on your planet are rectangle in shape. Is this some other dimension speaking to your world? Yes, it is.

As humanity evolves out of the prison mentality, you will see how fluid your world truly is. There are water worlds connected to your planet...fire worlds connected to earth and a snow universe tied to your dimension.

What are the triangle and box people trying to say to your collective?

Why do most of you live in a box-shaped house or apartment? The box is the most prominent shape on your planet. What are the box people saying?

Wake the hell up, humans.

Shape species connect to your planet to assist it as it evolves and returns to the astral realities. One day humanity will have a conversation with your home. Talk to the door and ask what dimension it comes from. Why did the door choose you?

The only way to free your society is to see the world for what it is.

Go even further. Why did you choose that particular restaurant or grocery store to choose your food? You might not believe this but the food itself was calling you to consume it. Ever have a conversation with a hamburger?

As you shift out of the third dimension, your reality will become more fluid.

In the early stages of your earth's formation, the design of your future was foreseen. The dimensions that create the objects on your planet, such as chairs and buildings, were connected to your planet.

Mother earth brought in the energies she felt fit. Mother earth and mother god are technically the same thing. Realize a building is a portal to another dimension, which is no different than trees or grass. Humans on earth are the most inter-dimensional beings on the planet.

A soul cycle that is constantly in flux.

Earth was created in the Narrow Dimension, a hidden universe that was not fully explored during its time. Pockets of energy that had never been experienced before were brought to this universe. Remnants of other universes mixed into one.

Seen as a black hole, to give you an example of what it looks like in the third dimension.

As the earth was being broadcast to the universe, it was created in the shape beings connected to the earth's consciousness, which at first caused a new wave of energy. This planet was something special.

It was like a chessboard with more layers that can extract energies to create new species that had never been seen before. New kinds of lizards and mice species were found on earth, along with new kinds of insectoids that had never existed before.

Realize these are all animals that formed with the earth and many are no longer here.

As humanity shifts out of the third dimension, the narrow dimension will become clearer to you. The shape beings are normally collectives. They stick together and create universes that will allow more movement and dimensional shifts.

Ever see a box planet or a pyramid planet in space?

The flat earth should get some attention. Earth connects to all dimensions. It's all shapes and sizes that modern science could never explain.

Think of a world of only objects. They are moving around as they please. You can say living the simple life. The conversation is another story. They absorb each other's energies. And when aliens connect to their worlds, all they see are objects everywhere.

Some objects are kind and some are not. Some like to play games with your technologies. Yes, you can get trapped on a planet like this. They have a way of opening your telepathic abilities to speak with you. Most shape worlds are kind, but some are not.

Shape beings can transform their energies so they look like the alien species that is visiting them. The design is in shape form, so it's not an identical copy.

Ever feel unwanted in a building or a house? Sometimes it is the building itself that wants you to go. A past life with a house that didn't go too well is very real.

The consciousness of the buildings on this planet is no different than the energies of nature. When people take mind-altering drugs, they connect to the outer dimensions that surround their planet or live within it.

A talking chair or talking wall shouldn't bring any kind of surprise.

The square and rectangle shapes are most prominent on your planet. Currently, this form fits right into the structures of your society. As the energies of your reality increase to the fourth dimension, a shift will occur. The way you live your life will alter. Living in a circle house.

Teleporting the structure to another part of your world will be quite easy.

The Human

To give you an understanding of the climate on your planet and why the world is the way it is today, it's because humanity couldn't handle its true gifted power during the ancient times. You've probably heard this before.

During the time of Atlantis, humanity had incredible power. However, the power was abused and then it was gone. Ever since the dying days of Atlantis, humanity has been preparing to retake its power.

Why all the negativity on the planet? The human is in training to regain its power.

All the negativity on the planet is there because humanity is regaining its ability to reconnect with the universe. The more the negativity, the more strength is built.

Everyone is in some kind of study. Regaining powers of incredible magic is intense and very difficult to handle. For example, say you created a city with your abilities. Then you see your lover with another person. Jealousy energies are ignited and you can't handle it. You cause harm to both individuals, thinking that was the right decision, or, going even further, erasing them from existence by harming their family. Why did that happen? Because you can do anything at this level.

Not to say all Atlanteans did this...but it did happen on a wider scale. Irrational thinking absorbed the Atlanteans to a degree of insanity. Destruction of the planet was inevitable during the ancient times. Instead of the planet being destroyed, Atlantis was erased from history.

Not entirely as many of you have noticed. The pyramids are a signature of what was a great power source; a relic to remind you of your ancient ways. Humanity built the pyramids and influenced new cultures of life.

Abuse of power was inevitable as the Atlanteans experimented with technologies and new living conditions. The human as you know it was the final experiment and made into the final product of human that you see today.

With the help of the Annunaki and other species, the new human was phased in – another high- powered human that couldn't handle its power. The only difference with this human was it could be turned off...and it was.

The current DNA within the human is still connected to Atlantean origins. The only difference is the majority of the power is on life support.

Humans that murder other humans are trying to reactivate themselves. Atlanteans had the ability to murder with a single thought. Humans were that powerful.

Are the reptilians truly manipulating humanity?

The manipulations are being allowed for teaching purposes. Attacks are also downloads, and being in this body is not easy. At this low dimension, nothing is easy. It's either this or humanity causing harm to other alien life.

Not everyone wants to cause disruption, but there is enough in this world that will. Look at the current environment of the planet – not always a friendly place. Humanity is learning how to be responsible with its power.

The current learning environment is needed and was never meant to be easy.

How many worlds did the Atlanteans destroy? A great deal of planets.

Is this a child race? Humanity is being treated like a child because it behaved very badly in the past. The majority of alien species do not carry this DNA-like mixture. Think of all the drugs on the planet, all mixed into one product. Possessing superhuman abilities and able to move though the dimensions without a problem; God-like abilities that can easily be used to disrupt other worlds and even with a single thought can cause weather issues on another planet.

In the third dimension, at least, life is hell on this world.

Humanity has the ability to repower itself. A gradual move into the higher dimensions is being utilized. The road to the fifth dimension is very possible.

Does humanity really want this power? Most aren't ready because of the current reality. This grade level is an introduction of what's to come. If you pass the test, you can have an upgrade. If you use your upgrade for abilities of abuse, you get downgraded.

Atlantis energies are everywhere.

So, basically, the oversoul has a reason for the conflict in your life. Realize that the negativity in your life is a teacher, if you like it or not. The reasoning of it will never be clear. What matters most is that you find peace with yourself. Can you be alone? Can you go through stress and not get angry?

All these life trials are to improve yourself so you can handle the higher energies. Those that get constant attacks are here to speed up the process of the teachings, even if they feel they didn't learn anything.

You dropped down into the third dimension to rise out of this dimension as a better person. Rise above the distractions and follow your heart. The oversoul allows these tests to improve the soul and create new soul contracts.

The major plan is never truly known. One test at a time and seeing the larger picture isn't too important at this time. Connecting to telepathic energies and a heightened awareness of your spiritual surroundings will improve over time. The idea is to break open the timeline and let in new energies; a break from the third dimension and allowing fourth dimensional energies to heal the dimensional divide. The disconnect from spirit and the awakening of the third eye will occur. A trend of being more aware of your spiritual surroundings will be an everyday occurrence within conversations.

Can I handle being an Atlantean again? Can I reconnect with the universe and serve it well by using my powers in a mature manner? A reconnect to the earth's core and a new belief system will be engineered. A new way of thinking will occur, with a clear understanding that the war among mankind is over.

The divide is no longer needed.

Realize that, as hard as it is to believe, everything in your life happened for a reason. The negative and the positive all have a place in your life. Does death really exist?

When the body breaks down and can no longer carry the soul, the soul is released back into the astral. So, in truth, there is no death. The soul lives on forever.

Alien Felines Aren't Always To Be Trusted

Felines came from another universe.

Breeding programs were spread across your galaxy, seeding new worlds with the feline experiment. Once the species is able to take care of itself, the parents leave for another world. And this goes on and on forever.

Do realize that not all the felines created are made with the best intentions. As are the reptilians, some felines are made to kill and conquer. With the assistance of genetic engineering, the humanoid feline is assisted until they can live life on their own, the same as the Homo sapiens.

There're always going to be different variations of feline, the same as humans on your world. Some worlds have felines very evolved who live in the fourth and fifth dimensions, and in some worlds, the felines go through the third dimension.

There are fish felines and dolphin felines, which are some of the most powerful beings in the universe. The dolphins are similar in advanced gifts to the feline. The sonar on a dolphin is similar to a feline's sense of hearing.

Higher senses are a necessity to soul growth, especially when the species is matured enough where it is then tested. A paradise world is nice, but it becomes a better, more fluid paradise when it is tested for its strengths. What is life without a challenge?

The planet Lyra that is no longer in the Lyra star system was one of those worlds that was heavily challenged. Known for their scientific breakthroughs, the Lyrans were a peaceful race. Yes, they had a rough past for soul growth, but they achieved peace within their race.

Similar to Atlantis, Lyra had its utopia. Power split through the feline religions that existed, causing a divide within the race. Religion was created for soul growth, and as your world, it got out of hand. The only difference is that the Lyrans handled it better than humans on earth. Of course, the manipulation wasn't like it is currently on earth.

The creators of these religions began warfare on the planet. Because they were not receiving the kind of respect they expected from the population of

Lyra, war broke out. If you wonder where the religion of earth comes from, you might be getting an idea of its origins.

Basically some of the Lyrans were like Scientologists. "Come to us to achieve great power. And once you understand these gifts, we own you." The war on Lyra went on for generations. And yes, canines were on this planet as companions and pets. They even had lizard animals on the planets also. We don't want to use the word 'pets', but to explain it we are using that word for the moment.

To sidetrack for just a second—the majority of the worlds have some kind of insect-like species. Many worlds have jellyfish that hover in the skies. It's actually a beautiful sight to see. It's like having the ocean in the sky.

During this time of war with the felines, the human was being created, the human as you know it. The skin structure and DNA is very different, but the five-finger human was being genetically created at this time.

The Nordics were created during this time. Many became Andromedans, but those you know of that affected your world were Aryans. Once again, many were positive but many became very dangerous as their species evolved. Notice how many of your religious leaders are white. It all comes down to the Aryans that were manipulated, but some felt this was their right to manipulate others. So they have no issue with their deceptive behavior.

The fight between the felines and the religious believers went on for centuries. The war did cause a divide, but both parties settled their differences and became a neutral world. Like earth, you have many people who are very kind and live in the heart, and there are others who live for themselves.

Those who are deceptive did cause disruptions across the universe. They lived on Lyra with the positive Lyrans, and both sides learned from each other. Although they did not have wars they did have disagreements, but the planet needed this for soul advancement.

Making peace with souls you disagree with shows character. Being able to live with everyone is not easy. Basically how it works is that there are places you just don't go, like a forbidden zone of the planet. You can go there, but just be aware of the consequences. There are neutral places on the planet where everyone can connect, and then there are very dark regions where you need to be careful.

Realize this is one perspective.

This group of feline Lyrans that attacked the reptilians on earth in the ancient world were from Lyra. You can say they wanted their own world. And earth in the ancient times had only insectoid beings flying around and fish living in the tropics.

The reptilians on earth were, for the most part, harmless, at least until the Lyran felines attacked with a vengeance. They wanted the world for their own. The war for earth began. The fight was to eventually destroy earth but that was prohibited by the Arcturians.

The reptilians lost the fight and went to Lyra and destroyed the planet. Not all reptilians wanted this war with the Lyrans, and peace was made. So making peace pretty much meant the fight was lost.

Peace also meant the reptilians had to welcome the felines. That didn't go too well, which caused the destruction of Lyra.

With the human being the perfect component to earth, it became an insult to other species such as the reptilians and the felines. The Andromedans are part of the human ascension project on earth along with the Pleiadians and the Sirians.

At this time the human experience was expanding. Humans on earth would further the human experience for all species. The Andromedans felt a lacking in their own experience, meaning there was much more to learn. A disconnection from spirit is an experiment that went terribly wrong on many worlds.

Much was learned from those experiences, and earth would be the extension of what was understood. Earth was the new paradise where the human would go to the next level of evolution. With disagreements with the felines and reptilians, the human evolved, ignoring the signs of another war.

The idea of humans being created for earth was an atrocity to the felines. War broke out with the creators for allowing humanity to prosper on earth. The founders of the human species were killed in the beginning. No human should be allowed on earth. What was allowed to be created was corrupted.

To evolve an alien species you have to experiment. To evolve at all, experimenting is essential. Individuals who innovate in technology and in the medical field are part of the human DNA experiments. If you have any kind of sense you were part of the experimental process, you probably were involved with world or other worlds.

Every being ever created is in involved with the experiment is some form or another.

The feline tiger is known to enable change throughout the universe. The fury of not getting what they want can cause a super charge of emotions that will speed up the evolution process of the universe.

Some alien beings do want to destroy the universe, and some have succeeded. The tiger feline was involved, but to fully succeed, they needed to combine their energies with another alien race, and one of the most popular is the Archon.

The karma that comes with destroying a universe is immense—to turn a god against his own creation. Breaking part a universe is unheard of, but then again, not at all. With the assistance of God, anything can happen.

With a destroyed universe, the particles go everywhere into other realities.

Now you might have an idea where earth came from. This planet is a fractal of other universes. And earth is the next evolution of humanity. Like the insectoid, the human will one day saturate a universe and be part of the new species that will be the next generation of human.

Creation is constantly improving itself. With the balance of dark and light, humanity will continue to evolve with all species of alien. University and universe sound the same, don't they? Universal knowledge is in constant flux.

If you can survive the boredom of everyday life on earth…you can pretty much survive anything.

Life of a Galactic Diplomat

Basically you surrender everything.

The ideas of a good life and comfort instantly fade until your mission is complete. Realize – many souls are trapped on earth through the reincarnation cycle. Trapped souls created the matrix, as you call it. Humans are used to keep the third dimension in its current state. The belief system is continuing the matrix agenda.

As a diplomat, you are here to assist with the transition into the fourth dimension by giving others the knowledge they need to transition. You are kind of like a galactic cheerleader, the only difference is that you are on constant attack, and yes, you have your days off but not many.

You make the choice to assist humanity on Earth because you have done this before on other worlds. In astral, you agreed to the assignment and made the transition to be prepared through various alien groups at the higher dimensions.

The last stop, before incarnating into earth to begin your diplomat mission, is the fourth dimension. There are different kinds of diplomats – some with family and others without. Those without are kind of undercover. It's like being a secret agent diplomat. It's best you go solo so you can concentrate on your mission.

To change the world, you need to be a little odd. This might be hard to hear, but the more comfort you have in life, the less likely you are to assist humanity; the more irritation, the better to complete your mission. Unfortunately, the more you don't like your life, the more likely you are to bring in the higher dimensions.

You are on assignment twenty-four hours a day. Instead of meeting up with friends at the local bar, you are channeling a mission, or assisting humanity in some way. You live a life in combat and, realize, you are undercover. There's no military badge or CIA briefing. As a galactic diplomat, you download information spiritually.

Astral is your contact and remembering your dreams is unlikely. Living on a planet that is under siege is no picnic. You have the channeled information you need for your mission, no more and no less. There's always more information you can access, but there is a time and a place for everything.

Life on a war planet is no easy incarnation. When you are here to assist, you will be moving through the dimensions. Some channelers are here to bring comfort and prepare souls for the next phase. As a diplomat, your life will not be easy.

Shutting down the third dimension is controversial, as it manipulates most of our consciousness. Some Orions are causing issues with the Earth's atmosphere. Reptilians from other dimensions want to cause suffering for humans because of their alien ancestors.

Humans are blind at the moment and one day they will see.

As a diplomat, you will feel the suffering going on around the world. The comforts of life are usually very distant – but that's the mission. There have been diplomats in the past, but many failed; once again, the comforts of life. Instead of going outward to assist, they follow the tradition of other channelers and healers and bring in no change.

Yes, there are reptilians that are disgusted with humans. Manipulating the timelines and causing mental issues is their pride and joy. Take advantage of the coward human and hurt them mentally.

The felines use humans to counter these attacks.

Join the army and fight in the wars. There is a war going on between the felines and the reptilians, and both are malevolent beings, dark fighting dark using humans as the puppets. Do realize that boredom creates a lazy human.

Laziness comes from the felines. This is used in several different ways, on of which is that it's there to combat stress by relaxing. Understand – just because you aren't in combat fighting a war doesn't mean you are not a part of it.

Everyone is involved.

Abuse of the human collective is felt throughout the human consciousness. You laugh together and feel pain together. When you are on a planet together, you are one.

Everyone on this planet knows each other. You might not want to know each other, but you are all connected from other lifetimes on other worlds. Remembering a soul from the spirit world isn't easy on a planet. But remembering a soul you knew from another world is very easy.

Many diplomats were terrible people in their past lives. Not all have been negative beings, but many have been. Those that have been dictators on other planets are perfect for assisting with ascension in a positive way, because they know how the dark operates. The problem is that when diplomats are assisting humanity, many remember that dark, past life and don't trust. Some understand it, and many don't want to understand it.

After being manipulated into war throughout human history, is humanity ready for peace?

Peace on the battlefield and peace at home are not the easiest transitions.

Understanding the fifth dimension is very easy. It's all the energies together. Your thoughts are in the mind of another. You have a thousand thoughts going on at once, and you understand each and every word.

Connecting to the divine energies of the higher spirit will assist with humanity transitioning into the fifth dimension. Ideas of the divine and a clear understanding of healing will begin to be felt worldwide.

All are healers on the planet. They just don't understand it at the moment. Look at how powerful words are. They can make you and break you.

As a galactic diplomat, you have to say what others to not want to hear and receive unwanted drama. Realize – you can be a galactic diplomat and have everything work out for you; have a family and live a positive life.

For those truly here to make a major change, they have to live in the warzone.

Live in a town you don't care for. Eat food you don't like, and live an unlucky but productive life. You can go through years of hell and not know your mission. When I say "years," that means 30 to 40 years of living not knowing what to do with your life.

When you get activated, you will know.

A turn of events, and you will just know what to do, whatever it might be. It could be channeling or healing. You might just want to write a book and have no idea where the information came from.

Knowledge is key to the awakening. Don't be afraid to put the information out there. There will always be those hesitant to channel and it's not always the right time to put the information out there. You will know when it's time to release this knowledge.

Blessings.

How Spirit Guides
Work Around You

This is a short overview of how the spirit world works.

For everyone the spirit world is unique in its own way. Not everyone will see the spirit world the same way. In the third dimension, you will realize there are all kinds of spirit worlds and definitions.

Some will call the spirit world the astral plane. Others would call spirit where you go after you die. Technically you are always in astral. Technically you are always in spirit. So when you die you are already there.

Your human self is just a fractal of your higher consciousness, which means you are everywhere in different universes in multiple realities at once. To connect to this energy in its entirety is almost impossible in this current dimension. Fragments of the information are possible to connect to. Knowing this world and how it works is most important.

Spirit guides are friends and family from other realities that exist in the spirit world.

To be clear, we are going to focus on the spirit world, calling that home. And when we say astral we are speaking of astral travel in the universe that is currently connected to your human perspective.

The spirit world is home and it's whatever you want it to be. Do realize just because you have everything you want doesn't mean your soul expands in such a place. It can, but your soul needs to be tested, and that is what the astral plane is.

So the spirit world is the higher dimensions. As for placing a number on the higher dimensions, that is impossible. Do realize humans on earth can reach the tenth dimension in your reality. Your consciousness is that powerful, but how long you can sustain that energy? For a long length of time can strain one's energy field.

Even in the third dimension one can reach the tenth dimension. Now this is rare, but it can happen and does happen but is not noticed normally.

Telekinesis power and flight can be connected to in the tenth dimension.

Basically you can have as many spirit guides as you would like. They are there to guide you with the information that is needed to utilize your journey on earth. Some spirit guides give you a few words and that's it. That's all you need is a few words of comfort.

You don't always listen to your guides so you have backup guides, and that can go on and on—backup for your backup basically. You tell your guides you are going to go to a dark place and you don't handle darkness very well.

That's why you are going there. It might take several lifetimes to dive into the darkness of the soul, but it's needed for soul growth. Souls that say they only have positive are hiding their darkness. Some are the most darkest beings you can ever encounter.

Like a vampire, they use devices to seduce their victims.

There is no such thing as all positive in all your world. There is a balance of light and dark, yes. Everything has light and dark; that includes God and your angels. It's not easy to anger God but it can happen.

In the spirit world negativity has no energy in the positive sectors of the spirit world. Those energies are not utilized. But there are negative areas of the spirit world you can go to that connect to astral.

If you want hell, you can have one. Some experience hell on earth because they need that experience. And some experience it on a daily basis because they feel it will bring in more strength.

Many doctors experience hell on earth by living in war zones.

Africa's energies are mostly coming from another planet. Africa is a healing center for souls that come from hell planets. There are so many parallel universes connecting to Africa, it's as if it's from another world.

The continent of Africa came from another world.

Your guides are family members, and yes, you can fire your family members. And sometimes those family members aren't good for your energy, but you wanted them around anyway, even if they ruin the party such as your life.

Do realize you can shut them down at anytime, but sometimes you need the teachings to better yourself. Or you have karma with that guide and you want to explore their energies by becoming similar to them in an earth lifetime.

Angels and guides can always be called on.

Angels are nurses, doctors, and counselors all in one. The archangels oversee what is happening on earth. So if you have any problems with earth, talk to them. After that long-winded conversation, they will connect you with the human consciousness.

They will tell you humans are learning lessons that your aliens will not learn. Some aliens like the fantastic, but many don't like to learn the hard lessons. That's why you are here to learn for them and help guide them. Many aliens can't handle earth; at least they don't think they can.

It takes a brave soul to come to earth. The darkness within does surface, but it can also be healed. Many beings aren't ready to face their darkness.

Live your life to its fullest and do the best you can.

There are multiple manipulations coming from Hollywood and Wall Street, telling you you need to be rich. You are rich, but it comes from within. Your inner power is your richness.

Inner beauty is more important than outer beauty.

When you discover these answers for yourself, you will have a better connection with your guides. The world will manipulate you as long as you let it. When you say stop, the energies will eventually clear.

As your energies increase in vibration, you will feel your guides, but you will see less guidance coming from them. Everyone has their own way of connecting to their guides, and some have no guides. Do realize the high council of the spirit world is always working through you.

Guidance can be coming from one universe or from another.

In astral, you can either talk to your guides or fire them. Astral can also cause difficulties for you to connect with your guides. It takes exercise to release the third dimension. You have to want to let it go for higher energies to come through.

If this is the world you want, the guides can have difficulties connecting with you.

This is why so many aren't aware of their guides. This dimension is working for them. Now you can enjoy this dimension and connect to your guides, but do realize the guide energy can be manipulated to fit this dimension, meaning some spiritual teachers see what they want to see.

A spiritual teacher can manipulate their own guides to fit their needs. What we mean as spiritual teacher is, someone who is aware of the higher energy presence. Spiritual teacher might make more sense than the word light worker.

The word light worker can be easily manipulated.

Do realize there are no secrets. There is no privacy. You can have privacy, but in the long run does it really matter? The spirit world knows the details of your private life.

This idea of working about the government spying on you–do realize the spirit world has been spying on you since your creation. Souls can be easily tracked, and there are no secrets.

The paranoia of third dimension will lift when you want it to.

It's up to the individual.

Spirit guides don't always agree with your decisions. When you go through a negative experience, they go through it also, and for some it hurts even more than it does for you. Guides can also cause you to make mistakes, and yet they are there for you to heal the mistake.

Some of you have contracts with your guides to go through their negativity, meaning you experience their mistakes and mishandling of your life. This is part of the life experience on earth and a spiritual awakening.

Connecting to parallel earth's moving the earth from the third dimension.

Awakening one's true happiness beyond material possession.

Material needs are a necessity, but what about the soul's energy and recognizing vibrations around you?

Humans are beyond alien. You are a spiritual force figuring out how to reconnect to the universe. Remembering your spiritual origins will take time. Connecting to the higher vibrations healing your daily life will help you learn new talents, talents you already know about but have recently forgotten due to this incarnation.

Guides are with you every day and every minute. They hear what you want them to hear. They do read your thoughts but only thoughts you want them to hear. Most just leave their minds open for the guides to see everything.

You are never alone. Your guides see your contracts, which are many. They see your entire life and have a good idea of where it will go even if you drift off into the wrong direction.

Your guides work through your thoughts to get you back on track.

The master manipulators want humanity to not know about their guides, not to know about the spirit world and the angelic realm. They don't want you to trust your psychic ability even if you use this ability on a daily basis.

If the word got out that everyone was psychic and that everyone uses these abilities on a daily basis, many wouldn't know what to do with themselves.

Do you want to heal the world and, most importantly, heal yourself? Then recognize your abilities and understand there is much more going on than this physical realm.

Angels and Demons

There is so much to understand about the angels; this will be a quick crash course. In the next book we will dive deeper into the subject matter.

Symphonic energy of the angels is love and light at a frequency that is not to be seen but to be felt. You can see the energies of the angels, but on this world it's to be felt. The angels connect you to other worlds and open you to other universes.

Angels can carry purses, and you can be in that purse just watching how they work. You can also dive into that purse and find yourself in another reality.

Humanity has connected to the lower energies and, to some surprise, the lower canine energies. When Sirius is spoken, the information about the Sirian canine is usually not mentioned. Just like the reptilians, the canines can be very vicious.

You want the lower dimensions and we will give it to you. The reason we are bringing this up is because it's never spoken about. Even humans do their own canine experiments to make a canine very beautiful or very vicious.

It's time for the earth to heal.

The angel energies are everything. Think of seeing the entire universe through a window. Every angel is a window to another universe. Every angel is a million realities going at a million miles per hour.

This is why so many souls have issues with patience. There is no need for patience in the higher dimensions. For worlds to be created in new ways, patience is needed. Patience is a calming energy, and it also gives the soul attention to detail. Patience is needed to be a better creator.

The life of an angel can be paradise or it can be hell. Some decided to be in the angelic realms at all dimensions, at the high and low dimensions. A third-dimensional angel is not easy because you know of the angelic realms, but you can't connect to them as you used to.

You can see other worlds but not understand your own. Archangels have mastered the lower dimensions and can balance the higher dimensions. You can see them as an army general if you like but not one to cause war.

There are billions of versions of Archangel Michaels and Gabriels and so on. Connect to the one that works for you. There are feline versions and Arcturian versions of Michael and Gabriel.

The Archangels in your Bible were the ones people found it easy to connect to. Their energies were everywhere, and those in need saw the archangels in several kinds of forms. The religions have humanized their energies, meaning Michael and Gabriel didn't exactly look human as you know it.

Connecting to the higher realms to assist humanity.

The consciousness of the Archangel energies can be interpreted in different ways, male or female. As you continue your connections with the higher realms, you will see all interpretations matter.

Archangel marriages and relationships are all possible with humans. Do realize there are trillions of realities, and everyone has had some kind of connection with an Archangel in some form or another.

The demons on your planet are from fallen angels. Once again, connect to your interpretation. Some of this information will not be easy, such as Jesus at one time being a demon. Another interpretation is that there is a version of a demonic Jesus on your planet, rising from the ashes and holding humanity hostage.

Jesus can also be connected to the Jinn because he was a Jinn in the past. That energy still persists on this planet, and once again this information isn't for everyone. When humans worship Jesus, they worship Jinn.

Not the most popular energy but very effective in the lower dimensions.

The astral realms connect humanity to the spirit world. At the moment the spirit world isn't always needed to be seen as humanity is coming out of hypnosis of the third dimension.

After the destruction of Atlantis, there were three energies of humanity: high frequency of the fifth dimension and third dimension and lower frequency of astral. The high frequencies had to be destroyed or removed because they were here in the physical.

High-frequency beings had to be erased from the planet because if they continued their stay, the earth was going to be destroyed. These high-frequency beings were around Egypt and Angkor Wat, to name a few of the sites.

Imagine Angkor Wat filled with color and of a high density with the energies of Tibet.

All of this had to be shut down for humanity to continue. Many years were spent hunting down Atlantean energies, and Egypt was the most destructive because the wars did cause flooding through Giza.

Egypt, the once paradise place of high vibration healing, shut down the lower dimensions of astral, where humanity was no longer able to connect with their guides and discovering alien beings was finding a god to worship.

The worship also was to lower the dimensions. The Greek gods were here to lower the earth's frequency. Not an easy decision but it had to be done.

With the earth's frequency so low, connecting to demons is very easy, and to understand their reign on your planet, even the aliens themselves get affected. Another name for earth is the tortured planet.

Shut off from the high dimensions, the aliens do what they can to assist to raise its frequency without being pulled into darkness. With humans being afraid of aliens, they send dark entities to aliens to attack them.

Angels have all the knowledge they need about you to assist in your incarnation. So the idea of privacy has been thrown out the window. They, like your guides, need to know you inside and out. They need to know your inner secrets so when you have a cold or an intense virus they can help you.

So basically the more they know the better. You give them these rights before you incarnate. Your guides and higher self can interfere if there is some kind of interference by another being.

Some beings such as angels and dark entities can interfere with you, and instantly they are attended to. Yes, some angels can go rogue. You know this before incarnating. Just so you know, before you incarnate the consequences are all understood. You might not like the contract and you must be mad to even consider reincarnating into a planet like this.

The disconnection from your guides is insane. Aliens have guides also but the connection is stronger. On earth the connection is at five percent or less. For aliens the connection is fifty to one hundred percent.

Every being in the universe has a unique relationship with spirit guides and angels. So to explain in detail of the relationships is kind of impossible.

Do realize demons incarnate as human for multiple reasons. Some incarnate to heal, even if they cause hell on earth. They are looking for a hug and someone to love them for who they are, and many wealthy people on earth are demons, and some are quiet and you would never know.

There are pleasant demons and nasty demons just like people on earth. It's just that demons have difficulty releasing their darkness.

Angels are similar as for personalities. Some are kind and others are ruthless in a nice way, meaning some angles can be cutthroat with their information. Like a hardcore teacher, they can carry a thick stick, but their intentions are to help you.

Angels are there to fire your guides. Angels remove the energies of the guides that were either lazy with you or just turned against you. Angels don't normally turn against the person they are protecting. But some do go to the dark side and become a fallen angel.

When the person they are protecting goes to the dark side your guides follow, and angels can also. You can inherit darker guides that will assist with your own destruction. Soul contracts can be changed, and going dark is an easy switch for some.

Continuing one's light isn't always that easy. Free will is such a powerful energy on earth. The spirit world is heavily tested by this world. The spirit world can be turned upside down by a human going towards the dark because so many timelines get affected.

What matters is surviving life. Recognizing your angelic energies will assist with your awakening. Everyone has been an angel spirit. This is your origin. What kind of angel you want to be is up to you–if you want to remember it or forget it.

For the human experience on earth, many forget their angelic connections. Connecting to your psychic abilities is your angel experience.

Enhancing the human experience on earth is what matters at the moment.

Do realize timing is everything as you connect to your higher dimensional self. You might be downloading too much of the human experience where you become depressed. It's not just your life you are connecting to but it's others.

Everyone on this planet wants to help others. Even those with dark intentions have a human heart of compassion somewhere. As you understand how connected you all are on this planet, life will simplify itself.

The Men In Black

Saving the best for last.

This book cannot be completed until the Men in Black (MIB) are mentioned. They have been on this planet for thousands of years. And yes... they work for the Illuminati, and, some say, there are agents that are Illuminati.

What is life like as an MIB agent? Basically, you have no life. Always working for the system, twenty-four hours a day. Most of it's technology work if it's not being manipulated by zetas. As you know, they work in the shadows and can appear anywhere.

MIB operate in the fourth dimension. The grim reaper, you can say, is an MIB agent. In the past, they appeared as demons. They can appear as anything. They wear black because in the 1920's, everyone wore black.

The style never changed and they can appear as FBI agents and be pretentious. They stay hidden for the most part and when they are seen, they look human. In the past, they appeared as monks and demonic beings to keep humans believing in the gods of their religions.

They appeared as demons but that doesn't mean they were ones.

As technology became more a part of the way of life, agendas were set to keep the UFO phenomena a secret. They can't do anything with Bob Lazar, because he has too much light on him. They can only handle isolated incidents.

Mostly alien sightings.

They don't normally wear sunglasses, because they interfere with their eyesight. The agents that are paired together connect through telepathy. They know each other's thoughts. It's as if they are logged into each other like a network.

Agents can break down and be decommissioned. The MIB movies are just a distraction and made to look ridiculous. So, when people hear about the MIB, they will say it's just a movie. It's another way to slow down disclosure – for now, at least.

Where do the MIB come from? We are made. We have our own planet in Sirius. Technically, we have planets everywhere, but we can't speak about that. We find it curious that humans want to talk to us. We are allowed to speak but that's about it.

We are a compilation of Zeta Grey, Reptilian, Pleiadian Nordic and other complicated connections we can't go into. Our planets are hidden because they were destroyed by the Nordics. We are the suppressors of all alien species.

We were made to be stealth and to continue the draconian ways of the universe.

We also know how the eyes and brain work, as you can see, appearing out of nowhere and removing ourselves from your vision. Just because we have disappeared doesn't mean we are gone. We are known to tamper with technologies, such as computers and mainframes.

The NSA hates us and the CIA adores us. We do things right and the reason the NSA hates us is because we know more than they do. Norad is another version of the NSA, except for the sky and outside the planet. The solar system is our home. We know what happens there. Earth is a boring place but the problem is when the solar system aliens come to earth with their agendas, we can't always keep them a secret.

The fires in California were a warning from an alien race. That's all we can say at the moment.

If you must know about our past, we have appeared on your world as monks, dark monks that come and go, removing thoughts and starting wars. We no longer have that ability. At the moment, we keep the aliens hidden from human eyes.

Yes, we are part of the secret space program, and yes, we disconnect channelers and computers if we must. Some of us are Martian, but not all. Mars is Earth's big sister. She has seen it all and Earth is about to get a major wake-up call.

Vortex's don't just open connections to other galaxies, they also open up to other universes.

If you want to find the Men in Black, connect to NASA. NASA's technologies interfere with the Earth's atmosphere and can cause earthquakes and other anomalies. As humanity awakens and changes the foundations of Earth's timeline, NASA will break down.

At the moment, NASA has humanity under lockdown. Notice how they don't really travel through space as you would think they would? NASA isn't interested in space – it is here to lock the planet down so humans can't connect to space. Makes sense, right?

Remember...they have a higher understanding of what is going on. They create the products humans use that shut down the consciousness of humanity. NASA mind controls agents and can be the masters of your mind.

The secret space program is plugged in and knows it, causing solar flares and memory loss. You can even blame cancer on it. You can technically blame all your health problems on NASA. One thing for sure – it is not here to help. If it was, you would be on the Moon and know more about the alien connections that are here on this planet.

The worst kept secret is alien life, and NASA knows it.

It programmed humans to be a slave robot society with fears and worries of the stock market crash. Problems everywhere, and NASA is a major link. The Illuminati are plugged into NASA. The Illuminati rule the planet from space.

Your alien rulers will come clean, over time, as humanity changes its ways. As humanity becomes more galactic, you will see the primitive ways of your world more clearly. And understand how your timelines fits together.

The MIB do not eat and follow normal practices. Some do, but most aren't interested in those experiences and find your human ways repulsive.

The MIB can manipulate the retina of the eye and cause mental health issues just by connecting to your eyes. It's a mental connection where the MIB can lock into your mind and shut you down. Put you to sleep wherever they might be.

They can use technologies to erase your mind, but they can just look at you and cause a loss of memory. Normally, they don't replace your thoughts with new ones. Your memory of events is just blanked out.

Understanding the MIB is like understanding all the alien species that connect with the Earth. Imagine alien catalogs, and the weaknesses of all beings, in a database on a computer screen. The Archons play a large role in corrupting connections and even shutting down MIB energies.

It's a hard game to play with the Archons because they seem to always win. This is why information gets out about UFOs. The Archons allow it to happen, along with other beings that won't be named. The spirit world plays a large role in the ascension.

The spirit world slowly allows alien information to be brought back to the earth. Malevolent beings can manipulate the information and suppress it, but that can only work for so long. And do realize that not all MIB personnel are negative enforcers.

Feel free to make your own choices but do realize we aren't all bad.

We go to work just like you, and we don't always like it. The only difference is that we are made in a high tech refrigerator, then cooked in an oven and – sooner or later – we get our downloads and are prepped for work.

We can die easily. One laser blast and we are goners. It really does suck to be us. The insectoids really give us a hard time. We can be taken over and used against reptilians. MK-Ultra, like you would never believe, is used on us.

What we see, our controllers see, also. You go on an interrogation, and it's like wearing a body cam. The only difference is that the body cam is inside your eyes.

Note: This was a rough text to channel because of the blockages around this subject matter.

The Awakening

Fifth-dimension awakening starts with letting go of the physical world. The future generations of your world will recognize the powers within. The Atlanteans wanted to let go of knowledge. The weakness within started this current earth, the hardships of negativity and illuminati mindset.

The ego has taken humanity into all kinds of different directions. The fear of your reality is so prominent and destructive to your society–a world without an identity. The ideas of slavery consume the human mind.

Once your planet sets itself free, connecting to energies and re-creating space travel, reinvention of society and how it thinks, creating new timelines of information to heal society.

Third dimension is an archon prison on your world, a fake world that calls itself real.

Connect to your spirit guides and realize they are real. They are friends on your spiritual path. As your DNA enhances and humanity connects from within to change timelines, the seed of your reality will shift to a higher dimension.

The virtual reality you are living in will begin to lower its frequency so you can see it better for what it is. As you ask for more information and to be free, the dynamic of the real world will come more clear.

Billionaires and those of the super rich know of the spiritual unknown. Not to say they fully understand it, but the idea of being free to do what you want is what they experience. The fragile nature of being free isn't taken for granted.

Imagine your entire generation of people being free to do as they wish every day. The positive nature of existence will become even more clear of who you truly are. Remove the stress and now you are free.

Humanity is treated like cattle on your world. The deceptive energies of manipulation run through your culture. Your job is your identity in the modern society. A job is to create income. But for most it is not an identity they really want.

How many people enjoy what they do for a living? Not many enjoy any of it. They might enjoy the rewards of being able to feed themselves and have shelter. The happiness level is very low. So the soul looks for entertainment.

The current entertainment environment is covered in illuminati manipulation, programming the human to be a zombie in the modern-day apocalypse. The modern family is broken. The modern life is backwards.

To move forward is to let go of the old programming. Look within and connect with your guides. Clear your guides and find an even balance.

Negative spirit guides run rampant on your planet. They tell you this is the right life, being a modern hippy with financial rewards. Materialism is king and everything else means nothing.

The life of luxury is a life of imprisonment.

Spiritual development is not easy on your world as the reptilians and archons tell you that you are bad. Humans are bad and so is spirituality. The rampant manipulation of the third dimension comes from all angles.

Understand that with your energies you can travel the universe. In your mind you can go there to a world of happiness. What is freedom to you? What is your definition of happiness? Let your mind fully connect to that vision and let it play out.

What is your ideal relationship and living condition? Go to your world of happiness, and in this place connect to the aliens. What your world will call aliens are, in truth, your galactic family.

How do you look in this world? Do you look human? What form pleases you most? Is it insectoid or is it feline? The more you know about your galactic family, the more you can add that knowledge to your own life.

This is medicine for the mind, creating a new reality of freedom and true free will.

If you were jobless for two years and without a care in the world, how would that make you feel?

You would have plenty of food and shelter that would give you comfort.

So being jobless for two years, we feel you would find something to do with your time. Feel the joy of doing what you want in life. Feel the love you would have for yourself and others. And most importantly, feel the gratitude you would have for being alive.

There is more, but that is all for now on this subject.

Printed in Great Britain
by Amazon